ST. PAUL'S LIBRARY

General Editors: THE REV. W. A. KELK
AND THE VERY REV. JOHN G. TIARKS, M.A., PROVOST OF BRADFORD

THE HOLY SPIRIT
IN THE LIFE OF TODAY

First List of Titles

THE MINISTRY OF THE WORD	F. D. Coggan
STRANGE VICTORY (HOLY COMMUNION)	M. A. C. Warren
THE BOOK OF COMMON PRAYER	D. E. W. Harrison
THE HOLY SPIRIT	F. W. Dillistone
THE CHURCH OF GOD	F. J. Taylor

THE HOLY SPIRIT
IN THE LIFE OF TODAY

By

F. W. DILLISTONE, M.A., D.D.

Author of *The Significance of the Cross*

General Preface by

THE LORD BISHOP OF SODOR AND MAN

THE CANTERBURY PRESS
LONDON :: EDINBURGH

THE CANTERBURY PRESS

LONDON: 33 Ludgate Hill, E.C.4
EDINBURGH: 31 Shandwick Place

First Edition 1946

*Made and Printed in Great Britain by Purnell & Sons, Ltd., Paulton (Somerset)
and London for the Publishers, The Proprietors of* THE RECORD, *Marshall,
Morgan & Scott, Ltd., 33 Ludgate Hill, London, E.C.4*

GENERAL PREFACE

THE Evangelical emphasis and interpretation in Christian theology for many years past has been voiced within the British Isles mainly by Free Church writers. It would be difficult to measure the obligation under which the whole Christian Church stands to thinkers like P. T. Forsyth, H. R. Mackintosh and J. S. Whale, among a host of others, for their witness to the Protestant and Evangelical tradition in Christendom.

Too little contribution, however, has been made recently by those who share the same tradition within the Church of England. For there is a distinctively Anglican interpretation of Evangelical theology, which needs to be emphasized if our Church is to fulfil the hopes which have been conceived of her potentialities in the great cause of Christian Reunion.

There is good reason to think that such a revival of articulate Evangelicalism would be particularly appropriate in the present phase of the development of Christian theology. The recovery of a more definite and authoritarian tone in the presentation of the full Christian faith, and especially the value now widely given to the doctrine of Redemption in the light of man's desperate need, has given new heart to those Anglican Churchmen who, while welcoming the freedom of thought and discussion which Liberal Protestantism has encouraged, have yet deplored its vague humanitarianism as a barren substitute for the full Christian Gospel.

16817

But there is a danger that this recent trend in theology is being exploited, on the one hand by the reactionary forces of Mediævalism and Ultramontanism, and on the other by an unreasoning Conservatism which applauds the

5

Barthian mistrust of all human endeavour mainly because it shrinks itself from the challenge of modern scientific thought.

It is all-important to maintain a right proportion between Traditionalism and Liberalism, and to retain, as far as possible, the advantages of both by combining single-hearted loyalty to the Apostolic Faith with " boldness to examine and faith to trust all truth".

Such a balanced statement of Church of England teaching, which is in the true succession with those religious leaders who gave us our Prayer Book and Articles, should be peculiarly pertinent at the present time. For the exigencies of a life-and-death struggle have indeed demanded the immediate replacement of what is obsolete by more efficient methods and instruments, but at the same time they have accentuated the value of those truths and qualities that have enduring worth.

Young men and women, with whom are the hopes of future years, will respect the Church that bears loyal witness to the eternal verities of her Faith, but they will also expect her to show her efficiency and realism by interpreting those truths in language that is both intelligible and relevant.

St. Paul's Library, therefore, does not consist of exhaustive academic treatises, but of a series of volumes of moderate length, which present Church of England teaching on the basis of an integrated Evangelical theology, expressed in a way that is readable alike to the intelligent amateur and to the trained student. While each author has been left entirely free to express his own opinions, for which he alone is responsible, it is hoped that the series will constitute a constructive and homogeneous contribution to Evangelical theology.

RALPH SODOR AND MAN.

PREFACE

A RECENT review in *The Times Literary Supplement* affirmed that " there are, perhaps, few Christian doctrines which are more perplexing to the average man than the doctrine of the Holy Spirit". I would like to think that this little book could prove of some service to the average man in his attempts to understand the doctrine and still more in his efforts to experience the power of the Holy Spirit in his life. In a very real sense it is to be regarded as a sequel to an earlier volume, *The Significance of the Cross*. It is built according to the same plan and seeks, as before, to lay a firm foundation for the building in the Biblical testimony. An attempt to justify this method of working will be found in the book on the Cross, but I hope that the sequel will make sense to those who are not acquainted with the earlier discussion. It is meant to stand by itself even though it is an essential part of its thesis that Pentecost presupposes Calvary both historically and experientially.

The book will always be associated in my own mind with the closing weeks of a most happy period of service at Wycliffe College, Toronto. The splendid library facilities, both of the College and of the University, were available to me at that time and greatly facilitated the actual shaping of the material which had accumulated over the years. To all my friends in Canada who helped me to know the true " fellowship of the Spirit " I tender my heartfelt thanks.

F.W.D.

1946

CONTENTS

The Holy Spirit " adjusts us to God".—*Irenaeus*.

" The Holy Spirit is the bond by which Christ efficaciously unites us to Himself."—*Calvin*.

" Effectual calling is the work of God's Spirit whereby, convincing us of our sin and misery, enlightening our minds in the knowledge of Christ and renewing our wills He doth persuade and enable us to embrace Jesus Christ freely offered to us in the gospel."—*Westminster Shorter Catechism*.

"Just this is the work of the Holy Spirit—to bring Christ into memory and glorify Him in us."—*Schleiermacher*.

" The echo of the word of Christ in our hearts, as the speech of God in us, is the Holy Spirit."—*Brunner*.

I

SPIRIT AND HOLY SPIRIT

> " There is another final Christian word, a word so
> dangerous that, for fear of misunderstanding, we
> may be tempted to banish it from our vocabulary :
> I mean the word ' Spirit '."
>
> SIR EDWYN HOSKYNS.

I

FEW words in use today cover so wide a range of meaning
as the terms ' spirit ' and ' spiritual '. They belong
to a class of expressions which, by very reason of their
lack of exact definition, form convenient labels to attach
to states of mind or feeling which can be vaguely discerned
but never exactly described. And man cannot do without
such words. The danger is, however, that he will use them
in an ever vaguer and looser way until they cease to have
any clear connotation at all and become mere conveniences
to cover up his own failure to observe accurately and
define precisely.

As soon as we begin to consider the word ' spirit '
our minds become conscious of an opposite over against
which it is usually set. For centuries, ' spirit ' and ' matter '
have constituted one of the great antitheses of human
life, and for many people today ' spirit ' stands simply
for that which is non-material, outside the realm of this
hard, matter-of-fact world in which we have to live. It
naturally follows that, inasmuch as during the past three
or four centuries material things have come to assume
an ever greater degree of importance in the minds of the
peoples of the West (and the same is becoming increasingly
true of the peoples of the East), ' spiritual ' things have
receded more and more into the background until in

many quarters it is being taken for granted that the 'spiritual' is simply another word for the 'unreal' and that if it comes to a choice between 'spirit' and 'matter' there can be no doubt about which must go to the wall.

Yet it is necessary at the very beginning of our study to challenge this assumption that 'spirit' and 'matter' refer to two quite different realms of experience. Professor W. MacNeile Dixon, in his Gifford Lectures, uncovers the issue in his own characteristic way.

" The word ' spirit '," he says, " is in our language and thoughts set over against matter and heavenly things opposed to terrestrial things. Yet this dichotomy is full of perils. On what grounds are terrestrial things so maligned ? And how do we know them or distinguish them from the superior things ? If I have, let us say, a liking for poetry or painting, am I spiritually minded ? Am I then on a higher moral plane than if my taste lies elsewhere—in travel, or mountaineering, or military history, or medicine, or machinery, or law ? Is mathematics a more spiritual exercise than flute-playing, or does social study give me a better chance of heaven than athletics ? Am I less spiritually-minded if I prefer the out-of-doors life, and am interested in plants and animals, than if I have a fancy for church music or high ritual ? Am I nearer God if I reflect on the mysteries of life and death than if I am immersed in civic and political activities ? . . . Things are by no means as simple as we are told " (*The Human Situation*, p. 221).

' Spirit ', then, we hold, is not just the opposite of matter and completely separated from it. At the same time there *is* a *distinction* between spirit and matter which we must seek to maintain. In general we shall regard ' spirit ' and ' spiritual ' as applying only within the area of conscious personal life. A lump of inanimate matter can hardly be called spiritual. It is true that a man whose vocation it is to deal constantly with inanimate matter can make of his work a ' spiritual ' pursuit, and it is true that matter in certain forms and arrangements can exercise a deep influence upon the ' spirit ' of man. Yet in both these instances it is not matter *in itself* which can be called ' spiritual '. When brought into relation with the conscious, experiencing individual it may be caught up into the realm of the spiritual and may actually form a channel or vehicle for ' spirit '; but apart from this context of living experience, ' spirit ' can hardly be said to exist. As our first conclusion, then, we would urge that ' spirit ' is not the mere antithesis of ' matter', but that only when matter stands in relation to an experiencing subject can it be spoken of as the agent of ' spirit ' or as the bearer of ' spiritual ' values. ' Spirit ', in fact, transcends ' matter ', but, so far as human experience is concerned, uses material means for its operation and self-communication.

II

Let us now examine certain uses of the term ' spirit ' and endeavour to ascertain what is its force in the general speech of our day. That it has an exceedingly wide range of meaning may be shown by reference to two books of fairly recent date.

In his valuable exposition of the doctrine of the Holy Spirit in St. Paul's writings, Mr. Birch Hoyle records, in his introductory chapter, some of the leading views which have been held about the nature of spirit. It is regarded as a semi-material substance, a kind of ' supernatural essence ' : or as a ' supernatural power ' sent forth from God : or as an immaterial supersensuous principle of existence : or as an instinct or influence in the hearts of men : or as a dialectical movement within reality itself : or as a common mind shared by a group of persons. Again, in his book on *The Spiritual Life*, Professor E. S. Brightman begins by asking " What is Spirit?",

13

and proceeds to set out a number of characteristics which may be regarded as the distinctive marks of 'spirit' in the world today. In the first place, he urges, spirit is conscious experience : nothing which is merely physical or material can be designated by the term 'spirit'. But more than this, it is experience which is powerful and courageous, directed towards the upbuilding of life as a whole, expressive of freedom and under the control of noble ideals : finally it is experience which is truly personal in all its manifestations. In face of such an imposing array of descriptions and definitions, the first reaction of the ordinary man is liable to be one of bewilderment. It is therefore desirable that we should first of all en-quire a little more closely into the connotation of the word 'spirit' as it is used in more popular speech at the present time.

First of all the word has been widely used to describe a common mind and outlook shared by a particular group of people. We find an author claiming that the British heritage is " a way of doing things in a certain spirit— a way different from any that has been given a trial before in the ordering of civilization". We find a journalist suggesting that the spirit of Paris is wiry and tough ; the German spirit heavy and brittle. In the latitude of the spirit it is farther from Berlin to Paris than from Berlin to Moscow or London. We hear the King, in one of his speeches, referring in glowing terms to " the spirit of the people ", which, though tested as never before in history, " burned like a bright flame, lit surely from those Unseen Fires which nothing can quench". To speak of the spirit of a nation or of a city is still a natural and meaningful form of expression. A bond of community, depending partly upon inherited tradition and partly upon experiences shared in common—such seems to be the meaning of 'spirit' when used in reference to the corporate life of mankind at the present time.

But the term is also used in connection with individual life. Let us consider a particularly vivid piece of writing drawn from the record of one who was doomed to endure the horrors of the concentration camp. Describing the journey to the camp, he writes :

" The hours dragged on as in an unshakeable bad dream. Somehow we endured—and I marvelled at the powers of endurance of human flesh. I remarked on this to Jan, who took exception ; ' *Despite* human flesh,' he said, ' man is sustained by the spirit '. And I must admit that he demonstrated his own theory, for he went through the ordeal better than most of us. At times he was even cheerful. But being in no mood to discuss metaphysics I must have dozed off—or lost consciousness—drugged by the torpor of the foul atmosphere and mesmerized by the constant clickety-clack of the wheels."[1]

Here there is something of the familiar antithesis between flesh and spirit, but that is not the main point of the extract. In this context, spirit stands for a capacity in man to lay hold of ideals, visions, hopes, which transcend and even contradict his immediate experience. The tortures and afflictions and despairs of the present he regards as the unreal, the promise of the future he regards as the real. Such a man, it is said in common speech, is upheld by spirit. A new power enters into him and sustains him, and for a time at least he seems to be living in a realm outside his immediate circumstances—the realm of spirit.

Let us take one more example from contemporary literature of the use of the word ' spirit '. In his striking book *The Predicament of Modern Man* Professor D. Elton Trueblood engages in a penetrating analysis of the ills from which our society is suffering and finally reaches this conclusion. " We need ", he says, " a world-shaking movement to offset the planetary dangers that a peculiar

[1] *Record of the Oswiecim Concentration Camp.*

combination of factors has now produced. What is required to save us from the destruction, of which world wars constitute a foretaste, is a new spirit. We need this far more desperately than we need any new machine or anything else. We are fairly clear concerning the nature of this new spirit, since it has been tested repeatedly in the religious tradition out of which our highest moral standards have come, even though it is now so largely ignored. We must spread this spirit by the written and spoken word, as many are already doing, though nowhere in sufficient force. But we must go beyond this to the formation of cells, made up of men and women who are as single-minded in their devotion to the redemptive task as the early Nazi party members were to the task of National Socialism " (pp. 96–7).

A new spirit! The words awaken an echoing response in our minds. A new direction, a new enthusiasm, a new motive-power, a new vision. For while the experiences of the past few years have made it abundantly clear that nothing can be achieved without due attention being paid to problems of machinery and supplies and organization of material resources, they have also shown that the final factor for consideration is the personal factor—the ' spirit ' of those who are to use the weapons and perform the technical tasks. So the ' spirit ' of the troops, the ' spirit ' of the workers, is a primary concern of those in authority, and the urgency of the need of a new ' spirit ', in face of the world problems which confront us at the present time, can scarcely be exaggerated.

Thus in the ordinary language of our contemporary world we find the word spirit being freely used. It denotes the bond of community which holds together a particular section of mankind ; it stands for the realm of hopes and ideals by which a man is sustained and upheld ; and it describes in a comprehensive way the direction and outlook by which men's lives can be guided and controlled. As we have seen, 'spirit' is not independent of outward forms and material resources; at the same time the all-important characteristic of 'spirit' is that it is not bound within the limits of that which can be determined by scientific means. 'Spirit' transcends the earthly and the visible, 'spirit' rises above the limits of space and time. 'Spirit' is still perhaps the best word which our language possesses for suggesting that there is a Beyond, an unseen world which is continually related to our own familiar experience but can never be finally contained within it. 'Spirit' is intangible and imperceptible but interpenetrating and powerful. To speak of 'spirit' is at least to open the door to another world.

III

There is, however, another term in our Western tradition which calls for examination. It is the term 'Holy Spirit'. What does this mean to the average reader or hearer at the present time? In one of his letters published under the title *Good News of God*, Professor Charles E. Raven refers to the Patristic doctrine of the Holy Spirit.

"The Spirit", he says, "became in fact little more than a convenient and impressive term for the magical powers bestowed by God upon the hierarchy and available with the appropriate ritual for their use. And do you think, my dear Henry, that the vast majority of our Church people have any very different notion today?

I don't believe they have. If one could look into their minds when they respond, 'Take not Thy Holy Spirit from us', would they, or for that matter the authors of the phrase, be able to give it any clear meaning? Doves, flames, seven-fold gifts which no one has ever classified intelligibly, gifts bestowed by episcopal hands—what sort of teaching does our Church give to interpret this medley of symbols? If we are honest, would not most of us have to confess that we are precisely in the position of those twelve whom St. Paul found at Ephesus (*Acts* 19 : 1-12), who did not so much as know if there was any Holy Ghost? And in consequence all this glorious knowledge that the whole creative process is the scene of His energy, that every least impulse towards fullness of life is linked up at every level with His majestic effort, that in us all, wherever men and women are loving and joyous and peaceful and brave, He is manifested, and that all our aspirations towards a truer brotherhood, a nobler community of mankind are acknowledgments of His leading—all this finds no place in the worship and witness of our Church.

Nor is it any excrescence or insignificance in our Christian faith that we are thus ignoring. It is in some sense the very keystone of the arch of doctrine that binds together all the rest into a solid structure. If the doctrine of the Holy Spirit be ignored, the doctrine of creation becomes merely the tale of a bit of carpentry, of a world knocked together by a craftsman out of material external to himself, and then left to run by itself; incarnation becomes a theophany, for if incarnation has no relation to inspiration and the indwelling work of the Spirit, then not only is the Creed (' conceived by the Holy Ghost ') meaningless, but all possibility of interpreting or imitating Christ becomes absurd ; and atonement becomes magic, for it is only as by the operation of the Spirit working in us we are made at one with the mind of Christ that the word has any realistic meaning. The doctrine is essential. We have mislaid and neglected it. We must repent."[1]

Without committing ourselves to agreement with all that the author writes about the manifestations of the Holy Spirit, we must at least allow that his point is well taken and that to the majority of people today ' Holy

[1] *Good News of God*, pp. 101-2.

Spirit' is an almost meaningless expression. It is, for instance, notoriously true that whereas Christmas and Easter still maintain a firm hold upon the popular imagination, the Pentecostal festival is almost entirely ignored. Moreover, while a belief in a transcendent God who is Creator and Father of all still exists in the hearts of many, and while there is a widespread veneration of Jesus even in the most unlikely places, yet as far as the Holy Spirit is concerned, there seems to be a sheer indifference to the whole conception, for it seems to have so little to do with anything that we know in daily life.

What, we may ask, is the reason for this strange aversion to the very idea of Holy Spirit? It is true that the word 'Holy' is not often in use, but at the same time men are not without knowledge concerning its meaning. In general, it may be said to denote some relationship to the divine. A holy man, a holy place, a holy day—these are all regarded as belonging in some special way to God and as different, therefore, from other members of the class to which they belong. Yet this is not to say that they are entirely different. The man is still a man, the day is still a day, but being holy they stand apart from other men and other days in virtue of their special relationship to the divine.

Now the same surely is true of Holy Spirit. There is no need for it to recede into the haze of mystery and unreality. Unless we are using words in an entirely arbitrary way, Holy Spirit must have certain affinities with 'spirit' of which we have already spoken: at the same time, inasmuch as we speak of *Holy* Spirit, we must maintain the distinction from spirit, used in the senses which we have earlier described. Thus 'Holy Spirit' stands apart from anything within our experience and yet is akin to 'spirit' to which we commonly refer: and it is precisely this tension between the apartness and the kinship which constitutes one of our main problems as we seek to make the doctrine of the Holy Spirit relevant to the needs and aspirations of the ordinary man at the present time.

It is this tension which is so vividly portrayed in the sermon from which the quotation at the beginning of this chapter was taken. In the view of Sir Edwyn Hoskyns, we who seek to understand the great words of the Christian vocabulary are ever walking on a razor edge. On the one hand we must not identify Holy Spirit with certain exaltations of our own spirits ; nor must we assume that a mere sense of social togetherness is the fellowship of the Holy Spirit ; nor must we regard human affection as just another name for the love of the Holy Spirit. But, on the other hand, there is a very real danger of an attitude of detached aloofness, of imagining that Holy Spirit has nothing to do with spirit in the ordinary sense at all. As Hoskyns says, are not certain movements of the spirits of men, even when they are altogether undisciplined, parables, witnesses, signposts by which we are led to conceive of the workings and operations of the Holy Spirit of God ? And if our spirits are thus related to the Spirit of God, do they not become more than parables and signposts and tokens and witnesses ? Do they not become in this relativity genuinely and essentially related to God, manifestations of His glory ?[1]

Our conclusion, then, is that spirit in the ordinary senses which we considered earlier in this chapter is not simply another term for Holy Spirit. ' Spirit ' and ' Holy Spirit ' cannot be regarded as identical, nor can the second be defined simply by reference to the first. Nevertheless it is only through some knowledge of spirit that Holy Spirit becomes meaningful to us at all. At least, as Hoskyns says, there are parables and signposts to be discerned in spirit which can help us to conceive of the nature and operations of the Holy Spirit, and it is with these parables

[1] Cf. *Cambridge Sermons*, p. 149.

and signposts that we shall be mainly concerned in this book. After a rapid survey of the Biblical evidence, we shall consider in turn certain ways in which spirit is manifested, and with these as our parables and witnesses we shall be in a position to speak more fully of the Holy Spirit Himself. Yet we shall never expect to reach finality. The Holy Spirit cannot be contained within any merely human descriptive categories. He is of God, Holy, and therefore beyond our highest knowledge : yet as He joins Himself even to us, we may show forth His Glory by the very words which we use to bear witness to His operations in the hearts and lives of men.

II

A BIBLICAL SURVEY

" The living Christ is the Yea to which the Spirit
says Amen ; the Yea and the Amen both testify to
the same unshakable promises of God."

W. M. HORTON in
Our Eternal Contemporary.

BEFORE proceeding to a more detailed examination of
the ways in which the Spirit of God is manifested
in human life, let us make a brief survey of the Biblical
data. We shall seek in the first place to determine the
meanings of the terms which the Bible uses and secondly
to sketch an outline of the historical revelation of the
Spirit which the Bible discloses.

I

In relation to spirit, the Biblical vocabulary proves to
be comparatively simple. The altogether important word
in the Hebrew is *ruach*, a term originally employed to
describe loud, violent breathing and frequently applied
to the wind which swept down the mountain gorges and
whirled across the desert wastes.[1]

There was something unpredictable and awe-inspiring
about this powerful unseen force, and it is not surprising
that the word *ruach* should have soon come to be applied
to any manifestations of power which seemed to be
supernatural in their origin. These, it was said, were
manifestations of a divine *Ruach*. God was in action :

[1] For an authoritative account of the use of *ruach* in the Old Testament
see Norman H. Snaith, *Distinctive Ideas of the Old Testament*, Chapter 7.

22

His energy was being revealed: it behoved men to walk carefully in the presence of His holy *Ruach*.

As time went on, the abnormal operations of the divine Spirit received less emphasis and more attention was given to God's ordered activity within His creation. This meant that the word *ruach* tended to lose something of its distinctive meaning and ultimately it become possible to use *ruach* both of the divine activity in general and of that part of man's being which seemed to be specially open to the invasion of the divine. God's *Ruach* was ever active towards man: man's *ruach* might at any time receive the energizing of that divine *Ruach* from above.

When the necessity arose for translating the Hebrew scriptures into the Greek language there was never any serious doubt as to what word should stand for *ruach*. In Greek, *pneuma* " meant something material, not something spiritual in our sense—properly, the breath, but then also, in poetry, the wind, and in the language of early physicists and physicians, a kind of invisible substance or gas which could account for various affections in organic bodies " (E. Bevan, *Symbolism & Belief*, pp. 156–7). The all-important thing was that it could stand for wind or breath and was therefore a ready equivalent for the Hebrew term which never ceased to be applied to these natural phenomena. At the same time, once *pneuma* was used in this way to do duty for *ruach* it was inevitable that it should take on the wider connotations of the Hebrew word, especially as employed in the context of the relations between God and man. *Pneuma* in Hellenistic Jewish or Christian circles of the first century of our era stood primarily for the dynamic activity of God, but also, in a derived sense, for that part of man's nature which could become the field of operation of the one divine Spirit.

Ruach and *pneuma*, then, are easily the most important Biblical words for our consideration, but two others should

23

be mentioned which stand on a somewhat lower plane but have a measure of significance for our enquiry. These are the Hebrew *nephesh* and its rough equivalent in the Greek, *psyche*. In *Genesis* 2:7 the result of God's breathing into man's nostrils is that he becomes a living soul (*nephesh*), and in the O.T. generally this word is used to describe the principle of life which man as man possesses, a life which may become merely sensual in its aims or which may, on the other hand, be more and more directed towards spiritual ends. In the N.T. *psyche* usually stands for man's conscious and purposive life as distinguished from the merely instinctive and biological. Man is bidden consider how far he will be profited if he gains the whole world and loses his own *psyche*. Thus *psyche* tends to emphasize the moral side of man's nature more than *nephesh* does; at the same time, the meaning of each focuses around the mysterious life-principle which has been given to man and which he has the responsibility of directing towards good or ill.

Thus, in the special field of our consideration, the Biblical language is remarkably consistent. Man is created a living soul (*nephesh*, *psyche*) with a flesh-body: these are not independent of one another and it is always possible for the soul to become enmeshed within the realm of the fleshly and sensual. But there is also the divine *Ruach* or *Pneuma* by which God is constantly acting towards the sons of men. This *Ruach* of God comes into contact with the *nephesh* of man and thereby the soul is attracted away from the flesh towards higher and nobler ends. In so far as a living response is made, the *Ruach* enters into man and it becomes possible even to think of man possessing his own *ruach* or *pneuma*. Yet this is not the characteristic witness of the Bible. Pre-eminently the *Ruach* (*Pneuma*) is of God and only by constant dependence upon this power from on high can man move towards the attainment of his true destiny.

Let us now pass on to examine the great landmarks on the highway of the Biblical record of the revelation of Spirit. For the writers of the Old Testament from first to last ' the Spirit' denoted *God in action in human life*. Only in certain late documents was the Spirit brought into relation with inanimate matter, and these references can be regarded as exceptional. In the vast majority of cases the Spirit is spoken of as entering into a man or resting upon a man or laying hold of a man or coming upon a man or lifting up a man—when Spirit is spoken of, it is God's invasive action in the affairs of men which is altogether to the fore. The point is well expressed by Canon Quick when he writes : " In connection with God, the word *ruach* always suggests energetic action rather than immanence. It represents an invasive, rather than a pervasive power " (*Doctrines of the Creed*, p. 275).

It is in the writings of the prophets or of those belonging to their school that the most frequent references to the Spirit are to be found. In the Priestly writings, the Law and its ordinances quite naturally occupy a place of greater prominence. For has not priestly religion ever relied more upon the static and the traditional and the ordered than upon the dynamic and the novel and the free ? And in any full religious life there is certainly a part to be played by the elements which priestly circles have stressed. Without a framework of Law and Liturgy, religion can easily disintegrate into incoherence and extravagance. Yet it is equally true that, unless priestly forms be constantly polarized by the fresh and vital religion of the Spirit, they become hard and sterile. So the prophet was a man moved by the Spirit of God to challenge all final dogmatisms or ritual-systems, to protest against any final acceptance of existing conditions and to bear witness to the living energy of God, which could break down and build up and, above all, could bring to men the power of a new Divine Life. Such a witness did not necessarily involve the use of sensational and revolutionary methods. Nor did it necessarily involve a break with all existing practices. But, generally speaking, when a prophet responded to the invasive divine Spirit and bore witness to God's designs and purposes for His people, there was bound to be change and reformation. No accepted standards or customs can be exempt from judgment when brought into contact with the light and the holiness and the energy of the living Spirit of God. Thus in the main the Old Testament is concerned with the way in which the Spirit of God broke into the lives of particular men, inspiring them with fresh vigour and summoning them to undertake new tasks in their contemporary world. These tasks might be seemingly destructive or plainly restorative : each in its own way could serve as a manifestation of the judgment and mercy of God.

As the great days of prophecy drew to a close, two tendencies appeared within the life of Israel. On the one hand, there was the tendency to assume that the formative period of the nation's religious history was now past and that the living religion of the Spirit could be perpetuated within the fixed system of sacrificial worship and legal observance. In so far as the Spirit was still regarded as operative, it was as providing guidance and wisdom to those who occupied positions of responsibility in the institutional religious life of the people. On the other hand, there was the tendency on the part of some to look forward with eager expectation to a new and overwhelming manifestation of God's power, bringing to an end the existing order and inaugurating a new era of righteousness and peace. In their thought the new age would be ushered in by an unparalleled outpouring of God's Spirit, bringing gifts of prophecy to old and young alike, and making possible to all and sundry such a knowledge of God as they had never imagined before. It is against the background of this second outlook that we shall set the coming of the Messiah, as it is recorded in the Gospels of the New Testament.

There is, it has been pointed out, one major contrast between the New Testament doctrine of the Spirit and that of the Old. " In the Old Testament ", writes Canon Quick, " the Messianic connections of the doctrine are dim and slight. In the New Testament, on the other hand, it is broadly true to say that there is no teaching about the Spirit of God except in direct connection with the life and work of the Messiah Jesus " (*op. cit.*, pp. 276–7).

This statement is certainly true so far as the explicit references to the Spirit in the O.T. are concerned, though it must be remembered that it is not easy to define precisely the nature of the Messianic hope as it was held in Jewish circles in the centuries immediately preceding the Christian era. As we suggested at the conclusion of the preceding section, it was within the apocalyptic movement of late Judaism that hopes of a new outpouring of God's Spirit sprang up, and it is in the same context that we find the Messianic expectation most firmly held. However, so far as explicit references in the Old Testament are concerned, we have only two which associate the Spirit definitely with the figure of the Messiah. The first is in *Isaiah* 11 : 1–4.

" A shoot will spring from the stem of Jesse
And a sprout from his roots will bear fruit
And the spirit of the Lord will rest upon him
The spirit of wisdom and understanding
The spirit of counsel and might,
The spirit of knowledge and the fear of the Lord,
And his delight will be in the fear of the Lord.

27

He will not judge by that which his eyes shall see,
Nor decide by that which his ears shall hear ;
But with justice will he judge the needy,
And with fairness decide for the poor of the Lord ;
He will smite the ruthless with the rod of his mouth
And with the breath of his lips will he slay the wicked."
(*American Translation.*)

This is a notable passage which clearly depicts the work of breaking down and building up to which men are inspired by the Spirit of God. The Messianic King will be actuated by the Spirit to an outstanding degree and he will then become the perfect instrument for the fulfilment of God's mighty purpose.

The second example is to be found in *Isaiah* 61 : 1-3. " The spirit of the Lord God is upon me ; because the Lord hath anointed me to preach good tidings unto the meek ; he hath sent me to bind up the brokenhearted, to proclaim liberty to the captives, and the opening of the prison to them that are bound ; to proclaim the acceptable year of the Lord, and the day of vengeance of our God ; to comfort all that mourn ; to appoint unto them that mourn in Zion, to give unto them a garland for ashes, the oil of joy for mourning, the garment of praise for the spirit of heaviness ; that they might be called trees of righteousness, the planting of the Lord that, he might be glorified." (R.V.)

Here again the tasks of executing vengeance upon evildoers and of comforting those in distress stand side by side. The Messiah, acting under the constant influence of the Spirit, is to succeed in overthrowing the powers of darkness and bringing in a new age of liberty and joy.

There is still one other passage in *Isaiah* 42 : 1-4 where the Servant is endowed with the Spirit for his task of bringing justice to the nations. This section, however, was never regarded by the Jews as referring to the Messiah, though it becomes of real importance when viewed within the synthesis of Messiah and Servant which Jesus Himself effected.

Taking the Old Testament as a whole, then, we are bound to admit that the references to a Spirit-filled Messiah are only ' dim and slight'. Yet the Isaianic passages to which we have referred are full of significance, especially when we find that Jesus Himself regarded two of them as finding their fulfilment in His own Person. At His Baptism, words from *Isaiah* 42 were addressed to Him, and in the Nazareth synagogue He took the great utterance of *Isaiah* 61 and applied it directly to Himself. Thus there can be no doubt that Jesus regarded Himself as endued in an altogether unique way with that Spirit of God which had operated so mightily through the leaders and prophets of ancient times. They had received the Spirit in varying ways and in differing measures. They had been given commissions to perform, tasks related to the particular needs of their own times, and the Spirit had made them strong to obey. But no prophet would have regarded himself as able to speak words and perform actions which would be determinative for every age and generation. Jesus' acts were the evidence of the present reality and activity of the Kingdom of God. His words are never to pass away. No wonder that the Bible speaks of Him as possessing the Spirit without measure! By the Spirit He overcame the powers of evil, by the Spirit He performed works of healing and mercy, by the Spirit He proclaimed the Gospel of God, by the Spirit He lived in communion with His Father. In Him the Spirit dwelt fully. In Him we see a human life completely yielded to the Spirit's sway.

But the uniqueness of the Spirit's relationship with Jesus does not consist solely in the fact that He performed His mission in unceasing dependence upon the power from on high. As the Fourth Gospel clearly indicates, not only did the Spirit operate without hindrance in and through the humanity of Jesus: the day was to come when the Spirit would operate in an altogether new way within the fellowship which was to take the place of the humanity of Jesus after His withdrawal from the earth. It is not easy to expound *John* 7 : 37-9, but within the context of the whole Gospel it seems clearly to imply that it was necessary for Him who was full of the Spirit to pass through a perfected human experience, to suffer, to die and to rise again in order that the Spirit, which actuated His own humanity, might be bestowed upon the fellowship of those who allowed themselves to be drawn within the scope of His redeeming and sanctifying work. Only those who see in the cross of Jesus His final glory and triumph can receive His spirit. To be united with Him in His death and resurrection is to become a member of the Messianic community and so to receive the gift of the Spirit which the Messiah had the right to bestow upon all those who should believe on Him.

IV

As we pass beyond the Gospels, we find ourselves in the presence of an event of supreme importance. To the group of Jesus' disciples who were gathered together at the time of the Pentecostal festival, there came a soul-shaking experience which they had no hesitation in interpreting as the outpouring upon them of the Holy Spirit of God. The outward phenomena, however they are to be explained, are witnesses to the extraordinary character of the event and the subsequent behaviour of the disciples is sufficient testimony to its lasting effect upon their lives. They were convinced that their Master, Jesus, had been raised from the dead and exalted to the throne of the Messiah by the power of God. Being thus exalted, He had poured out His Spirit upon the members of His own community. They could now go forth in the power of that same Spirit to continue His Messianic work in the world.

This central claim of the *Acts of the Apostles* is fully supported in the later books of the New Testament. Take, for example, the *First Epistle of Peter*, a document which reflects the outlook of primitive Christianity whatever its precise date may be. In the fourth chapter we read :

" Inasmuch as ye are partakers of the sufferings of the Messiah, rejoice ; that at the revelation of His glory also ye may rejoice with exceeding joy. If ye are reproached for the name of Christ, blessed are ye ; because the Spirit of the glory and the Spirit of God resteth upon you."[1]

In this passage it is most impressive to see how closely the Messianic community is linked with the Messiah Himself. The community shares His sufferings, but it likewise shares His Spirit. Summarizing the meaning of this particular section, L. S. Thornton writes : " You are the Messianic community and you therefore partake of the Spirit which rests upon the Messiah. You are one with Christ in all things Messianic. You share the Name, the Glory and the Spirit. In Christ his people are one temple upon which God's Spirit rests, as the cloud rested upon the tabernacle in the wilderness. In this new sanctuary appears the glory of God which is inseparable from His Spirit" (*The Common Life in the Body of Christ*, pp. 37–8). During His earthly life, the Messiah Himself was the tabernacle or temple upon which the Spirit rested : now the community which is His body becomes His temple in the world and as such receives in outstanding measure that Spirit which rested upon Him.

The same thought appears in the *Epistle to the Hebrews* where those who had become partakers of the Messiah, (3 : 14), are reminded that they were also made partakers of the Holy Spirit (6 : 4). But it is above all, in the writings of St. Paul that the thought comes to full expression.

[1] L. S. Thornton's translation.

31

For him it was a fundamental principle that through the agency of the Spirit the graces and gifts of the Messiah were being reproduced in His people. Through the life, death and resurrection of Christ, a society had been brought into existence which could, without exaggeration, be called the very body of Christ. But upon this 'body', as upon the Messiah Himself at His Baptism, the Holy Ghost had been outpoured and the divine community had become the temple of God in which His Spirit dwelt. Thus those who became members of the Body of Christ through initiation into the Christian community, *ipso facto* became sharers of the Holy Spirit and entered into that fellowship of the Spirit which God had made possible through Christ.

As is well known, in St. Paul's writings Christ and the Spirit are so closely linked together that they seem at times to be almost identified with one another. But in the light of what has just been said this is perfectly understandable. For Paul was intimately acquainted with the Old Testament Scriptures and had knowledge of the Spirit of God before ever he came into contact with the Christian faith. Doubtless he had often pondered upon the living energy of God, the Spirit active in the affairs of men; doubtless he was aware of the hopes of the special outpouring of the Spirit which were associated with the Messianic age. When, then, the conviction broke into his soul that Jesus was truly the Messiah, that through Him God had visited and redeemed His people and had brought into being a new Messianic community for the fulfilment of His purpose amongst men, it followed as clearly as could be that God's living activity in and through Jesus was actually being continued in and through His Church. In other words, the Spirit manifested in the Messiah was being further manifested in the members of His Body. "In effect, he drew the Spirit and the living Christ closer together; he helped personalize the Spirit;

32

he ethicized the conception of the Spirit's operation; and he presented Christianity as the religion of the Spirit."[1]

What wonder that at times in St. Paul's writings it is hard to distinguish between Christ, the Spirit of Christ and the Spirit! The Christ in His incarnate life was certainly full of the Spirit: the risen Christ, he says, became life-giving Spirit: to be in Christ (in the Messiah) is certainly to share in His Spirit: to have the Spirit of Christ indwelling is to have Christ being formed in the heart and life. As Anderson Scott so well affirms: The Spirit in St. Paul's writings " has character and character which is known. It is in fact the character of Jesus of Nazareth. Whatever is known as to the purpose of His life, the relation into which He entered with men, the direction which His influence took, may equally be predicated of the Holy Spirit. In fact, as St. John afterwards averred that Jesus had ' declared the Father ' so St. Paul in effect assumes that He had revealed the Spirit ".[2]

It is perhaps in the eighth chapter of Romans that the connection between Christ and the Spirit is seen at its closest.

" But ye are not in the flesh, but in the spirit, if so be that the Spirit of God dwelleth in you. But if any man hath not the Spirit of Christ, he is none of his. And if Christ is in you, the body is dead because of sin; but the Spirit is life because of righteousness. But if the Spirit of him that raised up Jesus from the dead dwelleth in you, he that raised up Christ Jesus from the dead shall quicken also your mortal bodies through his Spirit that dwelleth in you." (R.V.)

As L. S. Thornton shows in his valuable exposition of the passage, it is possible to see behind St. Paul's words the recollection of the great promises of Joel where God had pledged Himself to dwell in the midst of His people

---

[1] A. M. Hunter, *Paul and his Predecessors*, p. 112.
[2] *Christianity according to St. Paul*, p. 144.

through His Spirit. "But," he continues, "the Spirit who thus comes to us from God is the Spirit wherewith according to his promise God has anointed his Messiah. He is the Spirit through whose agency all the promises of the old covenant have been fulfilled in Jesus. We receive the Spirit, not as individuals, but as partakers of the Christ, as members of the One Man in whom the whole purpose of God has been fulfilled. It is in this sense that a man 'has' the Spirit of Christ. 'If any man hath not the Spirit of Christ, he is none of his.' He belongs to the fallen race of Adam, not to the new creation in Christ. To partake of Christ and to partake of His Spirit are two sides of the same fact."[1]

Thus the general framework of the Biblical testimony is clear. 'The Spirit' is pre-eminently the title applied to God in action. Under the pre-Christian order, the Spirit came upon chosen men inspiring and constraining them to share in the divine activity in word and in deed. But this stage of the divine economy was not expected to continue indefinitely. A hope emerged of a new age when upon God's chosen Servant and Messiah the Spirit would rest in an altogether unparalleled way and when, to a far wider community, a participation in the divine gift would be granted. It is the universal testimony of the New Testament that all this has been fulfilled in and through Jesus. He, the Messiah of God, was endued with the Spirit and went about performing deeds of mercy and speaking words of salvation in accord with the mission to which God had called Him. Only through His death and resurrection, however, could His work be completed and the Spirit which dwelt in Him be shed abroad to wider circles of mankind. So He went steadfastly forward to suffering and death, confident that He was treading the pathway of His Father's Will. And so it proved. For death could not hold Him, and He being raised from

[1] *Op. cit.*, pp. 141-2.

34

the dead and exalted to His throne of Lordship, poured out His Spirit upon His expectant followers, constituting them thereby His own body, His Church, and bestowing upon them all the resources that they needed for their work and witness and community life. In this way there came into being the Spirit-filled community, sharing in the sufferings of the Messiah, but sharing also His Spirit and His glory. Henceforth it is the Church which is commissioned to perform divine deeds and speak divine words in the power of the same Spirit. So the Church lives, working and watching and witnessing in the Spirit, and rejoicing as she waits in hope of the Glory of God.

III

THE RESULTS OF THE SPIRIT'S ACTIVITY

(1) LIFE

" I believe in the Holy Ghost, the Lord and Giver of
Life."

The Nicene Creed.

" Spirit is not in the I but between I and Thou."

M. BUBER.

I

WHAT is Life? One after another of the mysteries of the universe has yielded up its secret to the enquiring human mind but this question still remains unanswered. Life can be recognized, life can be nurtured, life can be destroyed, but life cannot be finally explained. It is still true that the " capacity for correlation, persistence and individuality, for growing, multiplying and developing, for behaviour, experience and experiment which we call ' life ' . . . can nowise be explained in terms of anything simpler than itself " (*Ency. Religion & Ethics*, Vol. 8, p. 8).

Yet in the light of recent research it does become possible to gain a clearer conception of the peculiar characteristic of what we call ' life '. In the first place there is no completely isolated phenomenon which can be designated 'life' : in other words ' life ' only exists within a relation. One of the most fascinating attempts to describe the nature of life in popular language is to be found in Professor Erwin Schrodinger's recent book *What is Life?* and we shall quote a section bearing on this point. " What is the characteristic feature of life? " he asks. " When is a piece of matter said to be alive? When it goes on ' doing something ', moving, exchanging material with its environment and so forth, and that for a much longer period than we would expect an inanimate piece of matter to 'keep going' under similar circumstances. When a system that is not alive is isolated or placed in a uniform environment, all motion usually comes to a standstill very soon as a result of various kinds of friction ; differences of electric or chemical potential are equalized, substances which tend to form a chemical compound do so, temperature becomes uniform by heat conduction. After that the whole system fades away into a dead inert lump of matter. A permanent state is reached, in which no observable events occur" (pp. 70–1). Thus if life is to continue, exchanges must constantly be taking place between an organism and its environment : life can only exist in relationship.

In the second place, in spite of the widespread assumption that the existence of evolutionary development in the history of the universe has been proved (and there can be little doubt that over vast areas of observation the evidence is all in favour of such an assumption), it must be remembered that no direct link has yet been discovered between the realm of the non-living and that of the living. If, for example, we turn to the writings of Dr. Joseph Needham, the eminent bio-chemist, we find him laying the fullest possible emphasis upon the unity and the continuity which may be discerned within the structure and the history of the universe. Thus he writes : " In analysing the living body we come up from the ultimate particles, the protons and electrons, to atoms, from atoms to molecules, from molecules to the tiniest living particles, from these to cell-constituents, from cell-constituents to cells, from cells to organs, from organs to whole animals or to the whole human body. But why stop there ? Still further up, there are the conjoint realms of human mind, and of human society, with all its complex associations, reaching up from the family to the whole unity of mankind. So we recount our levels of organisation. Each is larger than the one before, but also essentially more complex and more highly organised. In terms of space, each contains the smaller one within itself.

"But space cannot stand without time. In every individual development, that of man no less than the meanest of them, the new individual starts at a low level, and climbs up to its perfection. But also we know without shadow of doubt that there has been, roughly speaking, in time, a development of stages of complexity and organisation similar to those stages which we see as we reflect on the make-up of the highest organisms. There was inorganic matter before there were worlds. There were worlds before there was life. There was some sort of primitive life . . . before there were plants and there were plants before there were animals. There were animals before there were men and there were men before there were those social organisms which we know as families and tribes. Then there came barbarous nations, and more civilised city states, and finally national states that we know to-day."[1]

But although it is possible to discern this remarkable continuity, it is equally possible to discern a remarkable discontinuity. The realm of the crystalline manifests many of the properties of a living organism, but it is not alive. The animal has much in common with man, but in the last resort there is a gulf fixed between the highest animal and the lowest man. Dr. Needham himself speaks of different *planes* or *hierarchies* or *levels* of organization and allows that whereas the stage may be completely set for the emergence of some new phenomenon, (if anything akin to what we call ' life ' was to develop, the environment in which it was to grow must needs have had the properties which it actually does have,)[2] it still cannot be proved that the stage itself produces the phenomenon.

[1] *This Changing World*, p. 37.
[2] Cp. J. Needham, *Time : the Refreshing River*, p. 258.

We are thus led to the conclusion that, whereas life in all its forms manifests a marvellous continuity of essential structure, with energy organized into ever more complex patterns, it is still impossible to explain life simply in terms of the inorganic which is below it in the scale of existence. In fact we may say that the question of the origin and nature of life is still an open one. It is entirely open to us to re-examine it from the point of view of the Biblical testimony. What, we may ask, is the Biblical approach to the mystery of life?

Before coming to the Old Testament, it will be of interest to glance at certain primitive ideas about the origin and sustenance of life. One of the earliest ideas, found in many parts of the world, is that somehow life is associated with and dependent upon breath. Man soon observed that when the breath departed from a body, life was gone; even when asleep he continued to breathe and it was only natural that by observing the rise and fall of the chest, or by experiencing the lack of breath after over-exertion, he should draw the conclusion that the breath was the very seat of life itself. Thus among the early Japanese, life and death were conceived as entirely dependent on breathing. The word for 'to live' is connected with 'breath'; the word for 'to die' seems simply to mean 'the wind goes' (*Ency. Rel. & Ethics*, vol. 8, p. 37). Among other peoples, too, the close connection between life on the one hand and breath or wind on the other may be readily observed.

This same connection may be found too, in the ancient mythologies and hymns of creation. A common picture is that of a deep abyss, dark and motionless, or of a deep valley between the walls of the hills, also dark and foreboding. Then the breath of the god or simply the wind begins to stir the scene and the possibility of life begins to appear. These primitive mythologies bear witness to man's close relationship with nature, and sex imagery may well be involved in the pictures just described. The important thing for us to notice, however, is the obvious kinship between breath and life and it may be added that this intuition of primitive man does come very near to the heart of life's mystery. Life, as we have noted, can only exist in relationship and except in the rarest possible instances (and even they are not certain) the environment within which life can continue must contain air for the organism to breathe. Thus if life may be said to depend on one thing more than another it is upon breath : and wind, air, breath, spirit may be said to constitute the essential principle of life.

When we come to the Old Testament we find a similar close connection between breath and life. In the opening verses of Genesis there is the picture of the Spirit (wind) of God hovering over the waters, though it is actually through the word of God that creation comes into exis-tence. But when the beasts and birds are spoken of (*Gen.* 6 : 17; 7 : 15) it is said that the breath of life was in them, and in the account of the creation of man (*Gen.* 2 : 7), the formative statement is made that God breathed into his nostrils the breath of life so that he became a living being. Whether there is any sharp distinction between man and other living creatures, it is not easy to say. Some would claim that there is, but on the whole it seems more likely that so far as the *natural* life was concerned, man was classed with the other living things. All life was derived from God : if He should take away His breath, death would inevitably follow and all things would turn again into dust (*Ps.* 104 : 29–30).

Thus in the general view of the Old Testament all natural life is of the same order, being derived from the Spirit of God (*Isa.* 42 : 5 ; *Zech.* 12 : 1). Yet it is not purely physical. The soul of man is part of his life and depends upon the life-breath as much as any other part. And still further the life of the social group depends upon the same breath which comes ultimately from God. So we may characterize the Hebrew view of natural life by saying that for them physical, psychical, and social life are all of a piece and that all come from the same source—the Breath or Spirit of God.

But this is not the whole of the Old Testament testimony about life. There is a remarkable passage in *Ezekiel* 37 where the prophet is taken out into the Babylonian plain and shown a vision of dry bones. They are very dry; they constitute the very symbol of despair and death. Yet in reality they represent the whole household of Israel, still alive so far as natural existence is concerned. But Israel has lost hope and is as good as dead. Therefore the prophet is bidden to prophesy to the breath :

" Prophesy, O mortal man, and say to the breath, ' Thus says the Lord God : Come from the four winds, O breath, and breathe into these slain men, that they may live.' So I prophesied as he had commanded, and the breath came unto them, and they lived, and stood upon their feet—an exceedingly great host."

The importance of this vision for our investigation lies in the fact that we find here a new conception of the nature of life. Life is not only something physical or natural, for the exiles were still alive in that respect. But they were without God and without hope, in the world. Cut off from a vital relationship with God they were as good as dead. But now it is the Spirit who is the giver of a new kind of life : life in relationship with God and with one another (22), life that is holy and pure (23), life that is peaceful and fruitful (26), life that is suffused with the presence and blessing of God Himself (27). Here then we have a new vision of what renewed and regenerated life may be. It is the same Spirit who is at work, but He

41

is working to the moral redemption and spiritual uplift of the people. The other references, in the later documents of the Old Testament, to the new spirit which is to come upon Israel belong to the same faith and witness. There is man's natural life which is created and sustained by the Spirit of God, but, still more, there is the life of personal relationship and moral growth which is also created and sustained by the Spirit, and it is this second quality of life which is all-important for man's present welfare and future destiny.

III

This vision of a renewed and purified people was one which never entirely faded out of post-exilic Judaism. Every school of religious thought sought in its own way to make ready a people prepared for the Lord. Some tended to withdraw from the world and to give themselves up to lives of strict discipline : others emphasized the duty and the privilege of the observances of religion and sought to foster a more worthy spirit of devotion and worship : others still (and these were the most influential) laid stress upon the Law of God as it affected every department of human life. They did not withdraw from secular affairs but made it their aim to perform every action in accordance with the rules and regulations revealed in the Law of the Lord. And they believed with all their heart that if only they could be utterly faithful in their observance of this Law, then their reward would be the supreme gift of life under the favour and benediction of God.

No man was more fully committed to this view than was Saul, a young Jew of Tarsus. Brought up within the strictest barriers of Jewish legalism, he became a zealous Pharisee and began to devote himself to a meticulous observance of the commands of the Law. This law, he firmly believed was ' unto Life ' (*Rom.* 7 : 10) ; he accepted without reserve the Jews' proud claim that it had the power of producing life, (*Gal.* 3 : 21, Moffatt's translation), that is, that it could bring the people of God to the final enjoyment of their promised inheritance. For Saul, like many other Jews, was not satisfied with the purely natural life : he desired, both for himself and for his nation, a higher form of life, eternal life, life under the direct blessing of God, life such as it had been portrayed by Ezekiel, life set free from the limitations of human suffering and mortality. And such life, he believed, would be granted both to him and to his fellow-Jews in so far as they proved themselves obedient to the righteous commands of God.

But Saul's beliefs and hopes were doomed to tragic disappointment. Gradually the bitter realization dawned upon his heart that instead of being the means of bringing him into fulness of life, the Law was actually shutting him up within the darkness of death. The seventh chapter of the *Epistle to the Romans* is the poignant record of his developing experience. There was a time, he says, when he was alive ' apart from the law '. He was living a purely natural life, care-free and irresponsible, enjoying in the manner of youth all the new experiences which the world had to offer him. But he could not remain for ever in that state. Aspiring to a higher form of life, he chose the Law as his guide to its attainment. And in a measure the Law was able to give him stimulus and help. But it was when the Law gave a command which he found himself unable to obey that Saul began to taste the bitterness of disillusionment. The more he struggled to rise, the deeper he sank into despair. The Law to which he had looked for life was actually proving to be the minister of Death. For sin in the flesh, which until the Law came, had been more or less quiescent, now sprang into life and Saul found himself gripped within the stronghold of Sin and its co-worker—Death. So the chapter draws to its close with an exceeding bitter cry : " Oh wretched man that I am ; who shall deliver me from this body of death ? "

The answer to this despairing utterance is to be found in the extraordinary exultation of Chapter 8, though the prelude to victory is sounded even at the close of Chapter 7, " I thank God through Jesus Christ our Lord." In other words, real life is to be found in a personal relationship. The amazing change takes place simply by the transference of expectancy and hope from the Law to the Christ. Thereby Paul finds himself living according to an entirely new principle. Instead of remaining in bondage under the law of sin and death (a law which had not been displaced but only fastened more firmly upon him by the Law contained in ordinances), he finds himself moving freely and purposefully within the sphere of life in Christ Jesus. What no legal system had been able to do for him, because of the fact that it was always dogged by his own inability to rise to the standard which it set before him, God sending His own Son into the very midst of the sinful situation, had triumphantly accomplished.

The succeeding verses of Chapter 8 expound more fully the nature of this new ' life ' in Christ Jesus. Supremely it is life in the Spirit. Ezekiel's vision has found fulfilment in reality. The Spirit has come and breathed even upon those languishing under the tyranny of Sin and Death, and the result has been new life. Only it is not a vague and undefined life. It is life in Christ Jesus (2) ; it is life indwelt by the Spirit of Christ (9) ; it is life quickened by the Spirit of Him that raised up Jesus from the dead (10). Expressed in another way, it is life within the family of God. " For as many as are led by the Spirit of God, they are the sons of God. For ye have not received the spirit of bondage again to fear ; but ye have received the Spirit of adoption, whereby we cry, Abba, Father. The Spirit itself beareth witness with our spirit, that we are the

44

children of God : and if children then heirs ; heirs of God and joint-heirs with Christ ; if so be that we suffer with him, that we may be also glorified together " (14–17).

Thus for Paul the new life, life in the Spirit, begins, continues and ends in relationship with the living Christ. Through a personal relation with Him in faith, man enters within a new dimension of the Spirit's working. Life on the natural level is indeed dependent upon the Spirit, but the law of Sin and Death is such that unless a man consciously lays hold upon the Spirit's high resources in Christ Jesus, he is bound to be more and more firmly held within the prison which it creates. Let a man cast himself upon Christ, however, and he will be reborn into the new family in which Christ is the beloved Son : he will receive the spirit of Christ into his heart so that he may himself experience the life of sonship : and having thus received the earnest of the Spirit (2 *Cor*. 5 : 5) he can be confident that ultimately his own mortality will be swallowed up in the eternal life of the Kingdom of God.

Before concluding this short sketch of the New Testament view of Life, we may point out that the testimony of the Fourth Gospel is exactly in accord with that of St. Paul. In the Prologue we are confronted at once with the claim that " in Him was life " : every manifestation of life that we know is mediated through the eternal Word of God. But man through his blindness and ignorance shuts himself off from the source of life and walks in darkness and death. So the Eternal Life which was with the Father, was manifested in the world (1 *John* 1 : 2) and to as many as embraced the Divine Life, the right was given to become sons within the family of God (*John* 1 : 12). Thus the new life is a life in relationship with the Eternal Son and those who share it have been truly born of God (*John* 1 : 13).

This general theme of the Prologue is expounded more

fully within the Gospel itself and, in particular, reference is made to the Spirit through whom the life shared by the Father and the Son is communicated to men. In a measure the disciples were able to receive this Spirit even while the Lord was with them (14 : 17), for the very words which He spoke to them were Spirit and life (6 : 63). At the same time, the fulness of life through the Spirit could only be theirs after His glorification (7 : 39). His incarnate life had to be transformed through death and only then could He breathe on them and say, " Receive ye Holy Spirit " (20 : 22). Then, because He was already living in the order of the new creation, they also could live in the same environment (14 : 19), abiding ever in relation with Him who is the Resurrection and the Life (11 : 25). Thus, according to the witness of the Fourth Evangelist, true life, eternal life, is that which is in vital communion with the Father Himself. Such a communion, however, can only be known through the incarnate Son and can only be realized through the indwelling Spirit. We come back again to the outstanding principle of the New Testament—that real life only exists within personal relationships, and that because of the mission of the Son it is possible now for any man to enjoy a relationship with God Himself through the quickening influence of the Holy Spirit. " The union of the Christian with Christ in ' one spirit ' is the means whereby the whole koinonia of the Blessed Trinity becomes present in the regenerate life of man."[1]

IV

Let us seek in conclusion to gather together these various thoughts concerning life and the Spirit's relationship to it. In our opening section we drew attention to two points of emphasis within contemporary thought— that life depends upon relation and that life is to be regarded

[1] Thornton, *op. cit.*, p. 442.

as a unity. In our further discussion we found cause to modify these claims in one respect only. Life, we discovered, cannot simply be viewed at one level only. There are two levels or two dimensions to be considered—life on the natural level and life on the personal level, life in the realm of the senses and life in the realm of the imagination, life whose structure and order can be determined by scientific experimentation and life which is essentially free and whose structure can only be realized within the pattern of a personal life. Thus it follows that in regard to the first point of emphasis, relation must be viewed in two ways corresponding to these two levels of which we have spoken; and in regard to the second point, two unities must now be envisaged, the one natural and the other personal.

(1) *Relation*. That life exists in relation may be regarded as axiomatic, and this may be looked upon as the primary manifestation of Spirit. By a process which is still one of the ultimate mysteries of life, two cells come into relation with one another and thereby life comes into being. But the new living organism cannot exist in isolation. Only by a continuous interaction with its environment can it maintain a healthy life and become in turn the means of propagating further life in the universe.

Is there then any way in which the life-flow can be dammed and death can gain the ascendancy? There is at least one way, and that is by the strange process of Parasitism. Few terms in our language are more opprobrious than the term ' parasite '. Literally meaning one who eats at the table of another, it has come to stand for any man who maintains a soft and easy existence at the expense of another. But what is the phenomenon in the natural world to which the word is applied? In general it refers to any animal or plant, in fact any living thing, which sucks the life out of another organism without

47

contributing anything in return. It is relatively easy within the intricacies of nature for a small organism to gain entrance into the tissues of another, and it is when this happens, and the intruder takes advantage of his new position, that the process begins which may spell death for the host, while providing a temporary spurious life for the aggressor and invader.

In his exceedingly interesting article on this phenomenon in the *Encyclopædia Britannica*, Sir J. Arthur Thomson makes some remarks which are pertinent to our enquiry. " From a broad biological outlook," he says, " parasitism is a negative reaction to the struggle for existence and always implies the discovery and adoption of a mode of life that is nearer the line of least resistance. On this view the most diagnostic feature in parasitism is some retreat from strenuous struggle and independent endeavour." And again, " The most characteristic feature in parasitism is probably a kind of constitution more inclined to drift rather than to swim." He suggests that the motives, if such they may be called, which cause a living organism to behave thus are a love for the dark and hidden place, a desire for comfort, isolationism, a wish to escape from the struggle for daily food. And to give one more of his comments, the phenomenon is rare among types that breathe dry air.

All this is full of suggestion. It means, surely, that in every department of life the alternative to a truly relational existence where each gives to the other and receives in return, is parasitism. Whether life concerns plant and plant, or plant and animal, or man and animal, there must be the maintenance of true relations or deterioration is bound to ensue. This deterioration may take the form of enormity and flabbiness in the parasite or of weakness and debility in the host. In any case the relation has been disturbed, the Spirit has been spurned and life comes sooner or later to be destroyed.

It need hardly be said that what is true on the lower level is still more true on the higher level of personal relationships between God and man. The give and take of elementary forms of life here attains its fullest expression. When God addresses Himself personally to man and man makes response, then the new life of the Spirit is revealed and man may be said to be walking in the Spirit. But let him withdraw in any way into the parasitical attitude of which we have spoken! Then Spirit departs and man becomes unbalanced and retrogressive and the end is deterioration and death. Only in relation can the Spirit live.

(2) *Unity*. The infinite variety of organisms in the world sharing this one characteristic which we call 'Life' is in many ways the greatest marvel of the universe. Life *is* a unity. The same Energy, which we may now call the Energy of the Spirit, throbs through all, and even in the matter of organization there is much in common between the most complex and the simplest forms of life. Yes, and even on the higher level of which we have spoken, it is the same Spirit Who is energizing, and the pattern of His operation is not wholly different from that on the lower level of existence. Yet there is a difference. For the pattern of this new life after the Spirit is the pattern revealed in the perfect Son, the pattern of life which was laid down and taken again, the pattern of life renewed through death, the pattern of a love which gave itself to the uttermost, providing thereby both an unlimited succour and an absolute demand. This is the life of the new creation; this is the spirit of the new family of God.

So life on the natural level becomes love on the level of the new life in Christ Jesus. It was a mediæval saint who cried "He who loves not, lives not", and a more modern poet who wrote:

Not where I breathe
But where I love, I live.

The Spirit manifests Himself first as life but finally as love. It is through His energy that we live and move and have our being. Still more it is through His agency that our hearts are flooded with the love of God and we come to know that we have passed from death unto life because we love the brethren.

THE RESULTS OF THE SPIRIT'S ACTIVITY

(2) POWER

" Anyone who wishes to know the New Testament connotation of Spirit must use his concordance also for the term ' power ' which is its chief content."

JAMES DENNEY.

I

No problem has come to occupy so large a place in the public life of the twentieth century as has the problem of power. In international affairs there has been the struggle to maintain the balance of power : at the same time in- dividual nations have striven to be reckoned among the great powers of the world. In political affairs there have been bitter conflicts amongst contending parties and behind these conflicts there has lain the urge to attain power in order to be in a position to direct the life of the nation. In the economic world, centres of power have been established, the range of whose influence is literally stupendous ; there is little sign of any slackening of effort in the fierce competition for power in all its forms. The world of the twentieth century is power-conscious to an extraordinary degree. But although the problem of power has forced itself upon men's attention with a fresh insistence, it is obviously not an entirely new phenomenon in human life. In fact, as notable a thinker as Bertrand Russell has claimed in his book *Power* that man's whole life is controlled by a single urge—the urge to gain power and glory and above all to attain power over his fellow-men. All theories which suggest that man's primary interests are concerned with physical well-being, with obtaining food and clothing and the essential amenities of life, are, he claims, entirely wrong. Man's material needs can be satisfied but his lust for power can never be satisfied—it is insatiable. He uses his growing knowledge of science and techniques for the sole purpose of winning greater power. So this urge, carried to its extreme limits, brings about the insanity of the individual and even of a nation. The pursuit of power, in Russell's theory, is like a gold-rush : men forget all else as they go crazily forward to their ultimate doom.

As always happens with an over-simplified theory, it fails to cover all the facts. At the same time it is useless to deny that there are impressive elements of truth in this thesis. Striving after power *is* one of the fundamental instincts of the human heart, especially in the days of youth. In a valuable supplement (No. 212) to the *Christian News-Letter* on the subject of " *Christianity and Power* ", Dr. J. H. Oldham expresses the matter thus : " Power," he writes, " in its simplest meaning is the ability to do something or to act on some person or thing. As such it is inseparable from existence and life. To exist is to possess some measure of power, if only as resistance to the exercise of other power. All life is a manifestation of power, pushing its way forward, claiming room, seeking its place in the sun. Life is everywhere in competition with life. Growth takes place at the expense of other growth. This rivalry of power with power is fundamental to existence as we know it."

The struggle for power, then, belongs to the very constitution of human existence, and must not be regarded as wholly evil in its effects. A growing youth who struggles to attain his own self-hood and manhood, who aspires to gain strength in order to fight more effectively for a better world, is not necessarily guilty of selfishness or pride or other forms of wrong. Yet it must be admitted that there is scarcely any area of human life today where the possibilities of evil are so unlimited as in the field of the struggle of which we are now speaking. It is Dr. Oldham's judgment that the dictum of the late Lord Acton to the effect that "All power tends to corrupt and absolute power corrupts absolutely", has bitten deeper into the mind of the present generation than any text from the Bible. Quite certainly recent history has provided terrifying examples of the temptation by which man is continually assailed to use power for his own selfish ends, and for this very reason no Christian can afford to be indifferent to the problem of power as it presents itself before his mind today. " Power "—the ability to impose one's will on other human beings or to take decisions which will affect their lives—" is the great corrupter. It leads most easily to the worst abuses of the worst sin, pride. What feeds pride more fully than the ability to impose decisions on others ? What gives a man a greater sense of self-aggrandisement than the realization that other men must obey his will? Wherever the exercise of power is inevitable, the Christian conscience must be most alert and vigilant."[1]

We have said enough to show that the whole question of power is an utterly vital one in our contemporary world. Yet within the Biblical vocabulary power is associated again and again with the activity of the ' Spirit'. Can we then discover some fundamental relationship between power and the Spirit ? Can we through a true doctrine of the Spirit find a solution to the urgent problem of power ? In an endeavour to answer these questions, we shall first turn to certain records of man's primitive life and see how he regards power as it appears in its simplest forms.

II

It is a significant fact that Professor G. Van der Leeuw, in his massive phenomenology of religion entitled *Religion in Essence and Manifestation*, begins his exposition by devoting three chapters to the subject of ' Power '.

Religious experience, he says, is concerned with a highly exceptional and extremely impressive ' Other '

[1] *Christian News-Letter Supplement*, 190.

which forces itself upon man's attention. He recognizes the presence of this 'Other' primarily by the power which it generates. Taking this general affirmation as his starting point he goes on to show how this vague recognition of 'Power' is to be found in the most diverse parts of the world.

One of the most famous ideas in the whole history of anthropological research is that of *mana*. It was as long ago as 1878 that R. H. Codrington, a missionary to the South Seas, first mentioned the word in a letter and later defined it more precisely in his book on the Melanesian people. *Mana*, he wrote, "is a power or influence, not physical and in a way supernatural; but it shows itself in physical force, or in any kind of power or excellence which a man possesses. This *mana* is not fixed in anything, and can be conveyed in almost anything; but spirits . . . have it and can impart it. . . . All Melanesian religion consists, in fact, in getting this *mana* for one's self or getting it used for one's benefit."[1] Thus in the case of a warrior, if he is continuously successful in combat, he has *mana*; if on the other hand he suffers defeat, *mana* has deserted him. If a chief is wise and capable it is due to *mana*; if again he fails to hold his tribe together, it is because his *mana* has gone. "Power is authenticated by purely practical tests; in all cases whenever anything unusual or great, effective or successful is manifested, people speak of *mana*."[2]

Now it is a remarkable thing that similar words have been discovered in the vocabulary of other primitive peoples all denoting much the same thing. *Orenda* amongst the Iroquois, *wakanda* amongst the Sioux and *manitu* amongst the Algonquin Indians, stand for the same fundamental manifestation of power. The power may be manifested anywhere—in a stone, in a stream, in a tree, in an animal,

[1] Quoted Van der Leeuw, p. 24.
[2] *Ib.*, p. 25.

in man himself. Moreover, as man begins to make things he imagines that *mana* is to be found in his instruments of war or his domestic tools. In fact as Van der Leeuw suggests in a striking image, the primitive really interprets life " as a broad current " of mighty powers whose existence we do not specially observe, but which occasionally makes itself conspicuous by either the damming or the flooding of its waters.[1]

In other words, in the early view of man, power is a mighty force diffused throughout his universe. It may be stored up in a concentrated form in some person or object and in that case the person or object is a centre of danger to be approached only with extreme care : on the other hand, it may be released for human benefit and in that case it becomes a means of prosperity and blessing.

Thus in the most primitive forms of human existence we find man recognizing Power, desiring Power, sometimes afraid of Power, possessing only a dim consciousness of any personal nature of Power and yet aware that certain conditions must be fulfilled before any contact with Power can be established. By some it would be claimed that *mana, orenda*, etc., are wholly impersonal in their reference. But it is difficult to state the matter in this absolute way. There is, it is true, little suggestion of there being a direct personal agent in control of *mana* and directing its operations: at the same time, in view of primitive man's vivid sense of being related to the universe by which he is surrounded, it is hard to exclude the personal reference altogether. Through his experiences with *mana*, man learns a language which he can use when called upon to bear witness to those far greater events which happen when he is confronted by the living God Himself.

As we come within the circle of Biblical revelation we cannot fail to recognize certain impressive parallels to the primitive experiences of which we have just been speaking,

[1] p. 43.

together with certain radical differences. For instance there are undeniable similarities between the Hebrew *ruach* and the Melanesian *mana*. *Ruach-adonai* is certainly " the manifestation in human experience of life-giving, energy-creating power "[1] and at times it seemed to be purely physical in its manifestation. Yet the essential distinction is that *ruach* is the manifestation of the power *of God* and that normally, if not quite exclusively, this power operates in and through the lives of men. If we examine the places in the Old Testament where power is associated with the *ruach*, we find that the all-important consideration is that it is the Spirit *of the Lord* which is at work. When the Spirit came upon Jephthah (*Judges* 2 : 29) and upon Samson (*Judges* 14 : 6, 19 ; 15 : 14) the results were seen in intense and dynamic physical activity ; yet it must never be forgotten that they were agents, chosen by God to perform specific tasks on behalf of His people and that these outbursts of ' power ' were regarded as direct interventions of God to strengthen them as they threw themselves into the struggle. When further the Spirit came upon Saul so that he prophesied ecstatically and behaved in unusual ways, this, too, was regarded as an authentication of his mission and a sign that God was with him in his task of delivering the Israelites out of the power of their enemies. Time and again the Spirit comes with power upon the prophets (2 *Chr.* 24 : 20. *Ezek.* 2 : 2 ; 3 : 24. *Micah* 3 : 8. *Zech.* 4 : 6) and their resultant behaviour may suggest the presence of an impersonal *ruach*, controlling their lives. But when the whole record is read within its context we become conscious of a very different state of affairs. The central conviction of the various writers is that the living God stands over against all the evil forces which are seeking to dominate His people and lure them to their destruction. He sends His power upon both leaders and prophets in order that they may perform tasks beyond all normal human

[1]"The Doctrine of the Holy Spirit," *Headingley Lectures*, p. 4.

capacity, defying the powers of darkness and leading the redeemed of the Lord forth into the ways of righteousness and peace.

III

Passing over to the New Testament, we find an even greater emphasis upon the ' power ' which results from the activity of the Spirit. It is true that in the Synoptic Gospels *dunamis* is directly connected with the Spirit only by *Luke* (1 : 17, 35; 4 : 14). Nevertheless it might well be claimed that the entire Gospel story is in the nature of a commentary on *Acts* 10 : 38 where it is said that God anointed Jesus " with the Holy Ghost and with power ; who went about doing good and healing all that were oppressed of the devil ; for God was with Him." His words carried the unmistakeable note of authority and power. His healings involved the going forth of power as *Mark* 5 : 30 so vividly shows. It was increasingly recognized that more than human powers were at work in Him (*Mark* 6 : 14). And especially in the conflict with the forces of evil, it was through the power of the Spirit that Jesus gained the victory.

This last thought is brought home with great forcefulness in the parallel records of *Mark* 3 : 22–30 and *Matt.* 12 : 24–32 In these the Pharisees declare that Jesus is only able to perform his works of exorcism through the help of demonic influences. To this charge Jesus replies by pointing out that if a kingdom is divided against itself it cannot possibly stand. But he goes further. He insists that a supreme conflict is taking place between the kingdom of God and the kingdom of Satan. He Himself is leading the attack on the demonic powers through the direct assistance of the Spirit of God. " If I by the Spirit of God cast out devils, then is the kingdom of God come upon you." Nothing could indicate more clearly the way in which Jesus regarded His mission. The Spirit of God had come upon Him, and through this enduement of ' power ', He was able to declare war upon the forces of darkness. The very progress of the conflict was the sign that God's sovereign activity was at work in the world. The final outcome would be the destruction of sin and death, and the establishment of righteousness and life. In very truth Jesus' incarnate activity was a continuous manifestation of the ' power ' of the Spirit of God.

But all this was not to be brought to an abrupt ending by the death of Jesus. Instead, the Resurrection proved to be the supreme demonstration of the power of God through His Spirit (*Rom.* 1 : 4), and the ascended Christ could now bestow the same ' power ' upon His Church. " As if the Ascent of the Messias had opened Heaven, as if the Descent of the Paraclete had brought heaven out, the languages and habits of heaven seemed for a few years, a few decades, to hover within the Church after a manner hardly realized since, except occasionally and individually. There were miracles of healing and even miracles of destruction. In that first full vision and realization, powers exchanged themselves between believers. As in other great experiences, the primal sense of this experience renewed energies, more than mortal. At that time the Spirit in the Church sent through every power a double power, beyond their functions and their offices."[1] The speaking with tongues (*Acts* 2 : 4) the bold and effective witness which the disciples bore (*Acts* 4 : 31. 1 *Cor.* 2 : 4), the driving forth of evil spirits, the working of miracles, especially of healing (1 *Cor.* 12 : 10, 28), were all demonstrations of the Spirit and of power. The power of God fully manifested in the Messiah was now in divers ways pulsating through His Church.

Often today in Christian circles ' power ' is associated with the living of the good life, the attaining of a particular standard of individual behaviour. If a man reveals some

[1] Charles Williams, *The Descent of the Dove*, pp. 10-11.

obvious weakness of character he is bidden seek the power which comes from God in order that he may triumph over his disabilities. Now while in general this may be true to the spirit of the New Testament, it is not true to its characteristic use of the word power (*dunamis*). In the Gospels, as we have seen, the power of the Lord acting through Jesus enabled Him to defeat the devils, to heal men's diseases and to proclaim the Word of God. To His disciples also He gave power over all devils and to cure diseases, to preach the Kingdom of God and to heal the sick (*Luke* 9 : 1); on a notable occasion He assured the returning seventy He had given them authority over every power of the enemy (*Luke* 10 : 19). His final words as recorded in the Gospel are to the effect that all authority had now been granted to Him and that His followers had only to wait in expectancy and they, too, would be endued with power from on high.

In the succeeding books of the New Testament a similar characteristic use of the term ' power ' is to be found. There is the sense that the conflict between the Kingdom of God and the kingdom of darkness has reached its climax. In and through the resurrection of the Messiah the power of God's Kingdom has been revealed. Now, through the outpoured Spirit, the power is being plainly manifested in the very midst of human life. So the disciples receive power, the Holy Ghost coming upon them : with great power they bear witness to the resurrection of the Lord Jesus (*Acts* 4 : 33), many signs and wonders are done by the apostles even as they had been done by the Messiah Himself (*Acts* 2 : 22, 43) : with great enthusiasm, in spite of all the opposition of the rulers of the people, they speak the word of the Lord with all boldness. The same is true of Stephen (*Acts* 6 : 8), the same is true of Paul. In one of his outstanding descriptions of his missionary work Paul speaks of what Christ has wrought through him " by word and deed, in the power of signs and wonders, in the power of the Holy Ghost ; so that from Jerusalem and round about even unto Illyricum, I have fully preached the gospel of Christ " (*Rom.* 15 : 19-20).

A vivid illustration of Paul's conception of power is to be found in the opening section of the *First Epistle to the Corinthians*. Here Paul is concerned to set forth the true nature of his own mission and his great appeal is to the power of God which has been manifested at the very place where human weakness seemed most in evidence. The word of the cross, a word centring in a symbol of death and defeat, has proved to be the very power of God to those who are being saved ; the crucified Christ Himself, ridiculed by Jews and despised by Greeks, has proved to be the power of God and the wisdom of God. " Because the foolishness of God is wiser than men ; and the weakness of God is stronger than men." So Paul himself, though he had come in weakness and in fear and in much trembling, though his speech and his preaching had not been in persuasive words of human wisdom, had yet proved to be the means for the outward demonstration " of the Spirit and of power " ; in this way it was possible for the Corinthians' faith to be rooted not in the wisdom of men but in the power of God (1 *Cor.* 2 : 4, 6).

A further examination of St. Paul's Epistles shows how intimately in his own mind the power of God is associated with the resurrection of Christ. In *Phil.* 3 : 10 and in *Eph.* 1 : 19 ' power ' and ' resurrection ' stand together and, particularly in the latter passage, it becomes clear that for Paul the resurrection was the supreme manifestation of the energizing of God's power. He desires that his readers may know :

" What is the exceeding greatness of his power to us-ward who believe, according to that working of the strength of his might which he wrought in Christ, when he raised him from the dead, and made him to sit at his right hand in the heavenly places, far above all rule and authority and power."

In this passage words denoting might, energy, strength, power are all employed in the endeavour to show how great was the resurrection-victory of Christ; but the significant thing is that in the third chapter of the same Epistle there is a similar collocation of words when the application is being made to the inner lives of the members of the Church. Paul's prayer for them is that they may be "strengthened with power through His Spirit in the inner man". In other words his conviction is that the very same power of God which was active in raising Christ from the dead, is active within the Church to give believers the victory over every enemy—sin, death, the demonic hosts —which may be arrayed against them.

One final example of Paul's references to 'power' may be found in the concluding chapters of the *Second Epistle to the Corinthians*. In Chapter 12 he draws out once more the contrast between his own weakness and the power of Christ. Conscious of his own bodily infirmities, he is yet supremely confident that the power of the 'Messiah' is resting (the word used suggests the thought of the Shekinah in the Temple) upon his life. Though lacking in marks of outward dignity, he has yet shown all the marks of apostleship in his labours amongst the Corinthians—"miracles, wonders, and deeds of power" (12). And when he comes to them again to deal with certain sins and disorders in the Church, he is sure that his words will prove powerful and effective. For whatever his own weakness may be, he is a spokesman of Christ, and "it is no weak Christ you have to do with, but a Christ of power. For though He was crucified in his weakness, He lived by the power of God."[1] So Paul claims that the Corinthians will find that he, too, is alive by the same power of God. Nothing could make his thought clearer. The Messiah, in his struggle with the forces of evil in His incarnate life, had shown that the power of the

[1] 2 Cor. 13 : 3-4 (Moffatt).

Spirit of God was operating through him in word and deed. Even though it seemed finally that these forces had gained the victory over Him, yet out of that apparent defeat the most convincing demonstration of all the ages of the power and energy of God was manifested. And now that same power is at work in the Church and in the individual. In the struggle with all the powers of darkness, the victory of the Messiah is reproduced; out of weakness men are made strong, the power of the Spirit continues to operate, sin and death are overcome. This is the essential message of the New Testament, and it must constitute an integral part of any true view of the nature of the activity of the Spirit.

IV

So we come back to the problem of power with which we started. This is a problem which cannot be evaded, and yet it must be said at once that Christianity has no simple solution to offer. It is clear that man needs power in his struggle to live. In its most elementary form he needs power through food to provide him with energy for his daily tasks, and, if his own unaided strength is insufficient to gain the desired object, he must supplement his own power by powers drawn from the universe around him. He may enlist the help of a fellow human being, or he may invent a tool, or he may find some other way of harnessing the powers of the natural world to his own needs. But however it is done, power must be obtained if he is to continue to survive in a world where his energy is always wasting away.

What then is the specific Christian witness in regard to this problem? We would suggest that it is a dual witness —negative and positive, breaking down and building up. For in the first place the Biblical record makes it clear that the Holy Spirit has come with power upon chosen men, inspiring them to resist and bear witness against every form of tyranny which has sought to concentrate power in its own hands and to hold others in subjection and servitude. The concentration of power in the hands of a single man or a single group is always dangerous. It ministers to the pride and self-aggrandisement of the possessor of power and leads to the degradation and debasement of those who are enslaved. So the power of the Spirit of God is for the putting down of the mighty from their seats and for the exalting of them of low degree. This was supremely true of the Christ Himself, for by the power of the Spirit He set Himself to bring about the downfall of those powers which were tyrannizing over man, and to bring their captives out to a place of freedom and new life.

So it is the duty of the Church first of all to resist tyranny and overwhelming concentrations of power—be they political or economic or social—in the power of the Spirit of God by word and by deed. This may involve a major conflict with the State or with vested interests of one kind or another. Or it may involve an unfailing watchfulness, with a readiness to bear witness at once against any manifestation of overweening or tyrannizing power. This latter attitude is well represented in such a statement as the following, where Mr. T. S. Eliot seeks to grapple with the problem of power as it arises in the world today.

" There are several types of power, each with its own sphere ; and it is not healthy in a commonwealth, when any one type of power exercises unlimited sway—even if the centre of that power is denominated ' the people '. There is the power of the politicians, the power of the military, of the judiciary, of the various industrial, agricultural and other material interests ; the powers of the journalist and even of the artist must not be overlooked ; and finally the power of the Church. The areas are not clearly defined ; it is better that they should not be ; for in an active society, we must expect each centre of power to claim rather more than is appropriate to it ;

and the balance to be preserved by a wholesome contest. But in general it seems right that power should be specialized, and that those who exercise power in one sphere should *recognize authority* over themselves in other spheres. It is power arrogating other powers to itself, *power* in the generalized form, that arouses our most passionate sense of grievance."[1] Power absolutized—that is Antichrist, and against any such power the Christian must bear witness even to the point of suffering and death, in dependence upon and in the power of the Holy Spirit Himself.

But not only does the Spirit operate to the breaking down of tyranny and demonic worldly power. The Spirit brings power from on high to build up spiritual strength out of the very weakness and infirmity of human instruments. This is the altogether distinctive claim of the New Testament. It is that a power of a different order from that of all natural power comes into the world through the operation of the Spirit of God. It is possible to call it 'power', for it actually strengthens and invigorates men with divine energies, just as the agencies of the natural order revive the flagging energies of their physical life. Yet it is power from above, and as Paul insists, it attains its most signal manifestation when natural resources are utterly at an end.

This power is never to be employed in selfish ways. The very fact that it is given *through Christ* within His Church is a safeguard against any such use. For in Christ we see the power from on high directed towards the healing and saving and integrating of those broken and maimed by the struggle of life; we see the same power raising and restoring Him when the evil powers seemed to have Him within their grasp; and we see within the Church the continuing power of the living Christ setting men free and sanctifying them in body, soul and spirit, for the service of their fellow men. Moreover, the fact

---

[1] *Christian News-Letter Supplement*, 196.

that the power is always *from God* is a further and perhaps a final safeguard. For if this power is misused it will immediately be withdrawn. The power of God never serves to the glorification of man. But where man in his weakness seeks the glory of Christ and the upbuilding of the brotherhood—there the Holy Spirit enters and the Church is energized with the strength and power of the Almighty God Himself.

V

THE RESULTS OF THE SPIRIT'S ACTIVITY
(3) ORDER

"For God has not given us a timid spirit but a spirit
of power and of love and of discipline."

2. *Tim.* 1 : 7. *Moffatt.*

"We must still claim that Christianity enables us to
'make sense' of the world, not meaning that we can
show that it is sense, but with the more literal and
radical meaning of making into sense what, till it is
transformed, is largely nonsense—a disordered chaos
waiting to be reduced to order as the Spirit of God
gives it shape" ARCHBISHOP TEMPLE.

WE TURN to another problem which is causing men
deep concern at the present time : it is the problem
of the establishment of a true and lasting order in the
relations between individuals and nations, the construction
of the framework of a just and durable peace.

Under the stress of war conditions, it is not difficult
to create closely-knit communities inspired by a spirit
of harmonious co-operation. Thus a reviewer writes :
"Because of a common danger and a common task, men
on R.A.F. stations are an extraordinarily close community.
After a night's operations the crews may dash into a
neighbouring town to see a film or visit a friend, but this
contact with normal humanity is superficial, haphazard,
ephemeral, compared with their relationship to one another,
cemented by difficulties and dangers shared, and pervaded
always by the consciousness that death is close to them,
as it could not be to their fellow-citizens."[1] But how can

---

[1] Reviewer of Lord David Cecil's book on the R.A.F. in *The Times
Literary Supplement.*

this spirit of harmony and discipline and co-operation be carried over into days of peace ?

I

The problem becomes the more acute by reason of the fact that for better or worse the day of the small society has definitely passed away. Modern techniques—the radio, the press, speedy communications, the scientific management of large-scale organizations—have made the great society not only possible but inevitable.[1] And it is far more difficult to establish order and discipline within a vast social conglomeration of differing backgrounds and traditions than it is within a small society which is already reasonably homogeneous in its structure. The world has already seen one way of achieving a temporary unity. It is the way of dictatorship, the way of force, the way of using the techniques of which we have spoken to create a vast impersonal machine in which every man must play his specialized part without cavil and without question. Outwardly such a unity is exceedingly impressive. It can operate quickly and smoothly, with singleness of aim and a high degree of efficiency. The problem of order seems to be solved. But as events have shown, it is solved at a terrible cost. This cost is no less than the virtual disappearance of the individual and the destruction of freedom. Except for the tiny minority of the dictatorial caste, individuals are mere ciphers, and as far as freedom is concerned, there is no freedom outside the will of the Leader. This attempted solution, in fact, leads to what Dr. Mannheim calls a Mechanized Barbarism, and it is quite obvious that it is one with which Christianity can have no part or lot whatsoever.

What then is the alternative to the way of the dictator ? The world is struggling, almost in agony, to discover the

[1] Cp. Professor Karl Mannheim, *Diagnosis of our Time.*

answer to that question. One thing is becoming more and more clear. The freedom to maintain a truly personal life must be safeguarded at all costs : at the same time some degree of large-scale planning must be introduced if chaos is to be averted. This concept of Planned Freedom (using Dr. Mannheim's phrase again) may seem at first sight to be in the nature of a compromise, and there is certainly always the danger that it may weaken into a loose association which is no order at all. Yet if the polarity be maintained and a strong emphasis laid, both upon organization and upon spontaneous activity, there is no reason why there may not be found, within this living tension, the immediate solution which the world needs.

This brings us to what is perhaps the most important question of all. Has the Christian faith any word to speak to this present situation ? Has it any concern with the establishment of a new order in the world today ? For at least two reasons it may be claimed that Christianity has a peculiar relevance, and these we shall seek briefly to set forth.

In the first place, as Bishop George Bell points out in his little book *Christianity and World Order:* " The Christian seeks Order ; peace being (as St. Augustine said) ' the tranquillity which springs from Order.' And by ' Order ' is meant ' a system of right relations' " (73). This stress on right relations is one which we have already encountered in our enquiry, but it is one which it is impossible to over-emphasize. For as Professor John Macmurray has reminded us, " The problem of our relations to one another is the primary problem of practical life and is the key to all the other problems. If we order our relations to one another properly other problems will fall into place and be soluble ; if we fail here, everything else will inevitably go wrong. This is the primary law of life and it is an inexorable law of Nature, as fundamental as the law of gravitation."[1] Order, then, depends upon right relations, and if there is one thing with which the Christian gospel is concerned above all else it is the establishment of right relations. Thus wherever Christianity is able to bring about a re-adjustment of personal relationships between a man and his fellow, it is making a contribution of no small importance to the wider establishment of world order with which we are concerned.

In the second place, moreover, it may be claimed that in its doctrine of the Holy Spirit, Christianity comes to grips with the very problem of the creation of true community which is now before us. The whole question of the relation between the Christian faith and the bases of corporate life has recently been opened out in a suggestive fashion by Professor Edwin E. Aubrey.[2] He believes that the major task of theology in the next fifty years is to work out " a critical Christian social philosophy " : such questions as the nature of the influence of the social order upon the theologian himself, the way in which thought on human relations is affected by basic assumptions about the nature of man, and the manner in which man is able to communicate himself to another, need careful examination. But there is also, he points out, the exceedingly important question of the relation of the Holy Spirit to the religious com-munity. That they have been most closely related in the history of Christian thought is perfectly clear. But how does the Holy Spirit create the religious community ? In what sense is the Holy Spirit the bond of union in the community ? What significance has the doctrine of the Holy Spirit for an ecumenical church ? These and similar questions press for an answer at the present time, and are vitally important for the construction of the Christian social philosophy of which we stand in need. " Is it conceivable ", Dr. Aubrey finally asks, " that here we have

[1] *This Changing World*, pp. 257–8.
[2] See *Journal of Theological Studies*, Jan. 1940, and *Journal of Religion*, Oct. 1941.

a doctrine which is the hub of the whole contribution of Christian thought to the cultural problem of our time ? "

We have said enough to indicate that there is a real connection between the problems with which the planners of social order today are confronted and those with which the Christian faith has sought to deal through its witness to the activity of the Holy Spirit. Let us now seek to examine in more detail the way in which the concept of order has emerged within the history of human thought.

II

One of man's earliest discoveries seems to have been that arbitrary and unregulated power spells chaos. He recognized the presence of power in the universe around him, he coveted the possession of power : but it soon became apparent that if every one was a law unto himself, if the individual claimed the right to use the power in his possession simply for his own advantage or for the advantage of those to whom he was most closely allied, then nothing but disaster could follow. So we find growing up within the earliest forms of civilized society parallel concepts expressing the idea of *regulated* power, of *controlled* behaviour, of action directed to the welfare of the society as a *whole* and not simply to that of an individual or a minority. In other words, a principle of social order appears and it is of great interest to see how in widely separated areas of the earth's surface similar words can be found all representing this same fundamental reality.

Possibly the two most familiar examples are to be found in the *Rita* of India and the *Tao* of China. "In early Hinduism that conduct in men which can be called good consists in conformity to, or almost participation in the *Rita*—that great ritual or pattern of nature and supernature which is revealed alike in the cosmic order, the moral virtues, and the ceremonial of the temple. . . .

The Chinese also speak of a great thing (the greatest thing) called the *Tao*. It is the reality beyond all predicates, the abyss that was before the Creator Himself. It is Nature, it is the Way, the Road. It is the Way in which the universe goes on, the Way in which things everlastingly emerge stilly and tranquilly, into space and time. It is also the Way which every man should tread in imitation of that cosmic and supercosmic progression conforming all activities to that great exemplar."[1]

But not only is this concept to be found in India and China. *Asha* in Iran, *Ma'at* among the ancient Egyptians, *Dike* in Greece, *Fas* among the Romans, all stand for the same general reality. In all probability these words were first applied to the regularities which may be observed in nature—the movements of the sun and the stars, the succession of the seasons and so on. These were no manifestations of arbitrary power : rather they were evidences of a single order to which all phenomena were made to conform. If then the ground of the universe is orderly, men must behave in a similar fashion : it is an easy and obvious transition from the cosmic law to some form of elementary moral discipline. In other words, in the view of the leading thinkers of the ancient civilizations, community could only be established on the basis of the principle of Order which forms the very ground plan of the Universe itself.

Passing to the Old Testament, we find that a word of similar import had become firmly established in the Hebrew language. This was the word *mishpat*. It means, says Pedersen, " the law for the actions of mankind . . . and not only the law of mankind ; it denotes all law, all lawfulness."[2] It stands for justice and right in the widest sense, what ought to be done in any given circumstance. *Mishpat* comes specially to be used in connection with

---

[1] C. S. Lewis, *The Abolition of Man*, pp. 10–11.
[2] Israel, p. 351.

the Covenant on which the community life of Israel consistently depended. "This word is used to denote the decisive actions, by which a broken relation is established, the judicial proceedings as well as the word or act by which right is being recreated. But it is not the fundamental sense from which the others have developed. As directly derived from the root of the word is the significance of all the daily actions maintaining the covenant, viz., the true relation between human beings ; the word denotes what a man may claim and what he is to do towards others, or, in other words, the right and duty of everyone."[1]

What is peculiar about the Hebrew conception is that *mishpat* is regarded in no remote or impersonal way. Rather, seeing that *mishpat* is the ground work of the covenant, it must be regarded as upheld all the time by the direct action of God Himself. God maintains *mishpat*, and where any relation within the covenant is disturbed, he is concerned to recreate and restore it. Moreover in so doing he may act directly, but just as often he will operate through the mediation of human agents. And it is here that the Spirit comes into the picture. Men are endued with the Spirit in order that they may establish order and harmonious relations within the covenanted community. A few examples will readily make this clear.

No more vivid illustration can be found than that which is provided by the eleventh chapter of the book of *Numbers*. Within the Hebrew community, strife and dissension have broken out, and Moses is at the point of despair. He cries out to God that the burden of the people is heavier than he is able to bear. In response God bids him gather together seventy men of the elders of Israel, men of responsibility and leadership, and bring them to the tabernacle of the congregation. " And I will take of the

[1] Pedersen, *op. cit.*, 350.

spirit which is upon thee and will put it upon them; and they shall bear the burden of the people with thee, that thou bear it not thyself alone." Thus for the task of 'judging' the people and maintaining right relations within the community life, the Spirit which has hitherto rested upon one man is bestowed upon seventy others in order that they may take their share of communal responsibility. A similar thought is found in *Deut.* 34 : 9 where, after the laying on of Moses' hands, Joshua is endued with the spirit of wisdom for the judgment and leadership of the people.

Further examples of men being inspired by the Spirit for the task of upholding the covenant, both in relation to the outside world and with a view to the establishment of inner harmony, are to be found in the stories of Othniel (*Judges* 3 : 10), Gideon (*Judges* 6 : 34), David (1 *Sam.* 16 : 13), and Zechariah (2 *Chr.* 24 : 20). But of even greater importance, perhaps, are those passages which look forward to the coming of a ruler who will establish a new harmony and order in the life of the community and bring into existence a new covenant in which righteousness and justice will prevail. If we look to the book of *Jeremiah*, we find there a great prophecy concerning the new covenant (31 : 31-4): God's law will be written on men's hearts and all will enjoy an unhindered fellowship with Himself. The agent through whom this new era will be inaugurated is called the branch of righteousness, for he will execute judgment and righteousness in the land. Turning back now to *Isaiah* 11 we find a further description of this branch which is to grow out of the stem of Jesse.

" The spirit of the Lord shall rest upon him,
   the spirit of wisdom and understanding,
   the spirit of counsel and might, the spirit
   of knowledge and of the fear of the Lord. . . .

73

> And with righteousness shall he judge
> the poor and reprove with equity for
> the meek of the earth."

Here, in unmistakable terms, the chosen ruler is endowed
with the Spirit for the task of administering *mishpat*:
through the Spirit, that is to say, right relations are restored
and a true order established in the earth.

III

In the Gospel story the special function of establishing
judgment within the community is associated with the
title 'Son of Man'. As 'Son of Man' Jesus has power
to forgive sins, to make decisions in regard to sabbath
laws, to set forth the true standard of righteousness for
the life of the community. This He does while still on
earth, but in the final issue it is He who will sit on the
throne of His glory and bring into being that new order
in which righteousness will fully dwell. But not only
does Jesus through His words and deeds bring the divine
judgment into human life. Through a special relationship
with a band of chosen followers, He brings into existence
a new community established on the basis of a new covenant. This community constituted his *Habūrāh*, an Aramaic
term in current use to describe a group of companions
who were sharers in a common life,[1] and out of this
Habūrāh there emerges the *koinonia* or fellowship of the
early Church. Thus as Son of Man Jesus does two things.
He bears witness to those principles of the divine order
by which alone life can be carried forward harmoniously
and co-operatively in the world: He calls into being a
closely knit band of followers who are to share with Him
His temptations and sufferings but are also to become
partners with Him in the task of bringing judgment to

[1] See J. W. Bowman, *The Intention of Jesus*, p. 222.

74

the world (*Luke* 22 : 28–30). In short, Jesus sets forth the *principles* of true brotherhood and at the same time actually *establishes* a brotherhood in which the principles are to be exemplified and revealed. "Ye are the salt of the earth : . . . ye are the light of the world."

And all this is in the power of the Spirit. In the Gospels there is indeed no passage which explicitly refers the work of judgment and of restoring right-relations to the operation of the Spirit, though in *John* 16 it is made clear that through the Church He will convict the world of sin, of righteousness and of judgment to come. What soon becomes clear beyond doubt, however, is that it is only through the Spirit that the true life of the *koinonia* can come into existence, develop and grow.

It will be well at this point to pause and ask what exactly is the connotation of this important word *koinonia* as used in the New Testament. In *Acts* 2 : 42 it is said to have been one of the characteristic marks of the early Church and the word is of fairly frequent occurrence in the Epistles. As to its meaning, it is impossible to add anything to the altogether exhaustive examination of the word and its cognates which has been made by L. S. Thornton in his book *The Common Life in the Body of Christ*. His main conclusion is that the primary reference of *koinonia* is to participation in the Spirit, the Spirit which flowed into the fellowship from Him who was its head, even Christ. We know from the Epistles, he says, "that the *koinonia* language covers a great variety of ideas. Yet all of these various ideas can be seen to be closely inter-related in the well-defined pattern of the common life, as that life was shared in fellowship. That life transcended the community because in essence it was a communion with Christ and with the Holy Spirit. On the divine side it was a mystical union with and participation in the life of Christ through receiving the gift of the Spirit. On the human side it consisted in a fellowship of brethren, whose mutual relations were transformed in quality and significance through the gift which they shared. All the characteristic activities of this fellowship are manifestations of these two fundamental factors, of this one complex yet simple whole with *its two fundamental aspects, the divine and the human.* Such was the *koinonia* to which the first Christians ' devoted themselves ' " (*p.* 76).

This *koinonia* is twice designated by St. Paul the ' *koinonia* of the Spirit ' (2 *Cor.* 13 : 14. *Phil.* 2 : 1) and in a famous passage (1 *Cor.* 12–14) he describes in vivid language what such *koinonia* implies. In a word it implies a rich manifoldness within a close-knit unity. The community or fellowship of the Spirit is neither a drab monotone, nor a clash of opposites : rather is it the revelation of a brilliant variety of colours, which are blended together in a perfect harmony. The background of this picture is actually far from pleasant. In Corinth there had evidently been constant friction and petty jealousies. There were cliques, factions and a pathetic striving after the more spectacular exhibitions of spiritual power. In dealing with this situation, Paul sets forth certain great principles which are essential for the establishment of a true community life.

(1) Behind all the diversities of spiritual activity there is one God, one Lord, one Spirit. The Christian society can only be held together in a true unity by a realization of this fact (12 : 4–6).

(2) The manifestation of the Spirit is always given with a view to the profit of the whole community (12 : 7). To use a spiritual gift for self-enjoyment or self-display is to bring to nought the very purpose for which the gift was bestowed.

(3) *All* members of the Christian Church were through baptism initiated into a single Body, which is the Body of the Messiah : and being thus initiated they became partakers of the One Spirit by which the Body is held

together and unified. The familiar metaphor of the Body is worked out in detail to show that the Christian society is not a machine, nor a mere conglomeration of atoms, but a living unity of inter-relationships, in which every member has a part to play in the service of the whole and is indispensable to the health of the whole.

(4) There is one gift—love—which is less spectacular than those of healing and tongues and interpretations, but which actually transcends them all. In fact, unless all are suffused by the spirit of *Agape* (Love), they profit nothing. Thus one final requirement is necessary for the establishment of community and it is the supreme gift of the Spirit : Love.

These then are the principles of a true Christian order. God, says Paul, in a memorable phrase, is not the God of confusion but of peace : in Christ Jesus the character of the divine order has been manifest, and in and through the Spirit that order is being established in His Body, the Church. God is not glorified by ostentation and display but rather by edification and comfort : therefore " let all things be done decently and in order" (14 : 40).

In concluding this section we may sum up the witness of the New Testament to this aspect of the Spirit's activity by quoting from Dr. Moffatt's Commentary on the key-passage of 1 *Corinthians*.

" Within the Church the Spirit is the uniting power, which overcomes all differences of temperament and education and endowment, not obliterating them, but combining them in a common, co-operative service of the fellowship. Hence it is not an intermittent power, not even an *esprit de corps*, but a constant source of health and vitality in the Body. The gifts of the Spirit are not the native powers and capacities of human nature ; although these enter into the particular endowments of individual Christians in the fellowship, they are taken up into the new life and heightened. . . . Yet all bear upon the common good, and all derive their value from love, disinterested devotion to the good of others within the community " (p. 183).

IV

In his book entitled *Heaven and Earth*, Mr. Middleton Murry devotes an interesting chapter to the consideration of " The Mystery of Order " as it appears in the writings of William Shakespeare. " There is", he says, " an intimate connection in Shakespeare's mind between social order and the moral law. A twofold stream descends from God—one of social order, diffused over society by the instrument of the temporal power, the other of moral order, diffused over society by the instrument of the spiritual power. These preserve humanity from the beast that lurks within it, and the world from chaos" (p. 73). Without necessarily accepting this theory of Shakespeare's in its entirety, we can yet see that our consideration of the historic development of the idea of community-order leads us to a somewhat similar conclusion. The statement that " a twofold stream descends from God ", is a pictorial representation of what we can hardly fail to recognize in history. For there is first the widespread acknowledgment that creation is upheld by a principle of order to which man must conform : there is second, the growing witness that a further revelation of the Divine order is needed if humanity is to be saved from the excesses and disorders into which it is all too prone to fall. Thus the twofold stream we might more adequately describe as the Order of Creation, which is imprinted upon the Universe by the Word of God and sustained by the Spirit's continuing activity ; and the Order of Redemption, which is revealed in the Christ of God and actualized in His Church also by the Spirit's continuing activity. The first corresponds to the ' social order ' of Mr. Middleton Murry's description, though moral values must be included within it : the second corresponds to the 'moral order', though this must realize itself in social forms. The 'temporal power' must include all human institutions which seek to maintain the Order of Creation amongst men : the 'spiritual power' must refer to the particular divine society through which the Order of Redemption is mediated to a disintegrating and disordered world.

This dialectic of the two activities of Creation and Redemption has received increasing recognition in recent theological thinking but it is far from easy to grasp firmly or to express clearly. The attempt must be made, however, as we conclude this chapter, to apply it to the particular concept of order with which we have been concerned. Let us approach it in this way. One of the simplest forms of order which we know is provided by man's activity of breathing. The slow rhythm of inhalation and exhalation is a striking example of man's ordered relation to his environment : if it becomes hurried or laboured, distress ensues. So it is not difficult to conceive this steady and regular movement of the breath as being essential for the maintenance of a healthy and even a happy life. But once this idea gains acceptance, it can easily be extended to wider realms of human existence. Natural phenomena may be regarded as controlled by the same rhythmic motion, and even the entire living universe may seem to be ordered according to this principle. As is well known, such a theory was actually formulated by ancient Chinese sages who imagined that the history of the universe consisted of a constant rhythm of expansion and contraction. Through the operation of the twin-principles, *Yin* and *Yang*, all life was sustained in due order and constantly renewed.

Now when a theory such as this has come to be regarded as an adequate account of the natural life of the universe, the next step is to apply it to the moral life of man. May it not be that the same Breath which produces rhythm and harmony in the realm of physical relations also establishes health and order in man's relations with his fellow-men? Is not the structure of man's social life determined by the same principle which regulates the natural environment in which he lives? There is every reason to believe that the answers to these questions are in the affirmative. Social life, if it is to continue at all, must be subject to certain rules and it is man's task to discover the law which must govern the community at any particular time and in any particular set of circumstances. In general, we may say that the law will be a rhythmic one, allowing life to swing between the poles of strict planning and adventurous freedom. This is the law of Creation and only within its ambit can society live.

But although this pattern is written into the structure of the universe, man is ever prone to stabilize himself in the vicinity of one or other of the poles. He seeks either to establish a rigid legalism, or to remove all barriers so that an unrestrained individualism may be allowed fullest scope. In this way the rhythm is broken and social life either begins to be throttled by the tyranny of law, or simply disintegrates through the conflicting forces of a selfish individualism. The order of the universe is a polarity of authority and freedom and at every stage of his development man must seek to conform his individual and social life to this pattern. But as is tragically clear, history records the constant breaking of the rhythm through the pride and selfishness of man, and the necessity arises for that New Order of Redemption by which the broken structure may be repaired and the true harmony restored.

As our study has revealed, it is the claim of the Bible that this Order of Redemption was foreshadowed in the lives of Spirit-inspired leaders of ancient times and was brought to full expression in the experience of Him whose life moved steadily and unfalteringly between the poles of reverent submission to the authority of God and adventurous purposeful relations with men. Such a life was a challenge and a rebuke to the legalism and individualism in the midst of which He moved, and could not fail to exercise a redeeming influence upon every section of society which it touched. But this influence was not to be confined within the limits of a single human life-span. Through death the Spirit of that life was extended to a wider community—a fellowship ordered and regulated according to the pattern revealed in Him. There is, on the one hand, the reverent submission to the absolute authority of God (*Acts* 4); there is, on the other hand, a "common spontaneous activity—which indwells all and in each is kept right by the influence of all and prolongs the personal action of Christ" (*Schleiermacher*); the activity, in fact, which within the *koinonia* manifests itself as *agape* or love (*Acts* 2). This community of the Spirit becomes henceforth the rebuke and the stimulus to all the wider social groups of mankind. It acts as the conscience, or to use a physical metaphor, as the lungs of society: it is the organ of the Spirit and as such the exemplar of the true order designed and purposed by God Himself.

Such a community has a function of peculiar importance to fulfil in the world today. The two horns of individualism and collectivism constitute a tragic dilemma within modern social life. The tension between those who desire to plan and those who desire to remain free is acute. Cannot the Church so regain its harmony and order through the renewed guidance of the Spirit that it may bring light to the world's darkness and lead men into "the tranquillity which springs from Order" which is the way of peace?

THE RESULTS OF THE SPIRIT'S ACTIVITY

(4) GLORY

" A work of Genius is a Work not to be obtained by
the Invocation of Memory and her Syren Daughters,
but by Devout Prayer to that Eternal Spirit who can
enrich with all utterance and knowledge and sends
out his Seraphim with the hallowed fire of his Altar
to touch and purify the lips of whom he pleases."

JOHN MILTON.

" We beheld His Glory. . . . full of Grace and Truth."

John 1 : 14.

I

BY a strange coincidence, this chapter is beginning
to be written on a day which may prove to be a
turning point in world history. It is the day on which
the world's press is telling the public of the first use of
the atomic bomb ; this is being acclaimed as perhaps the
greatest discovery that science has ever made : the possibilities for good and ill are being graphically described :
the common man is being confirmed in his belief that
in the hands of the scientists lies the destiny of the world.
Yet it is part of the purpose of this chapter to suggest
that the last word does *not* rest with the scientist and
that even on the ' natural ' level there is something more
important than all the discoveries which science can make.
We have spoken of life and power and order—all categories
with which science is perfectly familiar, and about which it
has much to tell us. But something more is needed. In a word
we need value, purpose, significance, fulfilment and these, by
its very principles of operation, science is unable to supply.

Let us consider the words of two recent writers who are deeply concerned about the present predicament in which man finds himself. Professor John Macmurray, having stressed in words which we have already quoted the absolute primacy of personal relations, goes on to say: "We have reached a point in history where men everywhere are beginning to think of the making of a world-community as a practical necessity. The development of this conviction lags behind the march of events. It is a matter of life and death already. The alternative is universal frustration and bigger and more terrible wars." (In the light of the discovery of the atomic bomb, these words become increasingly ominous.) "But we have hardly begun to discover what is involved in the task of unifying mankind. We do realize that Science has made it possible. But we have still to discover that Art and Religion have even more essential parts to play. Science makes the world-community possible only in the sense that it provides the indispensable implements and techniques for doing the job. But that does not mean that we will do it or even that we are the sort of people who *can* do it. If we cling to the old familiar ways of life ; if we are afraid to change our habits and our ideas ; if our imaginations are too sluggish even to conceive a world much different from the one in which we have been brought up, then we will only be able to use Science to prevent the unification of mankind and to destroy one another, very scientifically, in an effort to preserve our tradition. It is the function of Art in all its forms to stir our sleeping emotions, and to bring our imagination to life. Art is creativeness ; and it wakens in us the creative impulses and the desire to make new things in new ways."[1]

In his exceedingly impressive book *The Annihilation of Man*, Leslie Paul speaks in similar terms. Science, he points out, is all the time seeking to eliminate the personal

[1] *This Changing World*, pp. 258–9.

equation from its operations : the more the scientist is able to keep his own personality out of his work, the more his observations are likely to correspond to the true nature of the universe around him. But then man has energies within himself which are not satisfied merely by a cold and dispassionate examination of outward phenomena. " In science . . . the energies of the mind are concentrated upon the systems of research, judgment is suspended and the result, in a sense fortuitous, may even offend the preconceived notions of the investigator : in art and religion the energies of the mind are directed at the result. To put it another way, if science proceeds by separation, art and religion proceed by identification. The mind or spirit is projected into outer reality, is poured out into the universe to illuminate all by its light. In this activity the imaginative and intuitive functions of the mind are directed in a creative, synthesizing way, not an analytical way, and the result is an act of knowing in terms of the values of the spirit of man ; it is a willed act as the burning, concentrated perception of the artist is a willed act, the consequence of which when we approach the work of the artist in his mood and not in the mood of the scientist is to flood us with his vision of truth" (pp. 166–7).

What both of these writers are concerned with is the fact that the scientific method is incapable by itself of solving the human problem. Science can tell us the nature of the raw material of life and what can be done with it : but more is needed if we are to know what is really *worth* doing and if we are to be motivated to undertake the task. In other words, science can tell us much about the *structure* of life but by itself it can tell us little about the *meaning* of life. Herein then lies the function of the artist.[1]

[1] To speak of religion at this stage tends somewhat to confuse the issue : the religion of creation may well be regarded as part of man's artistic activity and it may be better to postpone the consideration of the religious issues until we come to speak of the outworking of Redemption.

He has the responsibility of setting before the imagination of his contemporaries true values and ideals which will enable them to use the resources at their disposal in a constructive and finally meaningful way. He must so attune himself to the universe around him that he becomes able to determine its innermost significance and to mediate his knowledge to those who, without some vision of reality, must inevitably perish.

This point is so important that we shall pursue it a little further. If we diagnose the mood of our age correctly, we seem to find a widespread feeling that art has a part to play in the life of society, but no sure conviction as to what that part really is. People are ready to respond to the emotional appeal which art in its various forms may make, but often the response is faltering or blind and there is little sense of what is creative and what is destructive in that to which they expose themselves. What then, we may ask, is the criterion by which true art may be distinguished? To answer this question we shall turn to a suggestive essay by Augusto Centeno which introduces a symposium by four American writers entitled *The Intent of the Artist*. " Art," he says, in a pregnant sentence, " is a symbolic possession of life. . . . Scientific truth has its opposite in falsehood, moral truth in the lie ; but art has for its two poles the significant and the non-significant or insignificant. And this significance is always a reference to possessiveness. A truth—moral, social, etc—does not become artistically significant until it has been possessed in feeling, in motion, in tone ; until it has been liberated from its close context into a larger sense of human *livingness*. . . . A mere description of unconverted, unpossessed reality cannot be a work of creation" (pp. 9, 19).

If now we understand this author aright we find him telling us that the essence of true art consists in the emergence of the significant through a symbolic representation of some aspect of reality. The artist does not simply seek to paint a picture which is "true to life" : an accurate representation of that kind can be made by any camera. Rather he seeks so to yield himself up to his subject that he both possesses it and becomes possessed by it until finally its meaning grips his soul. Then, in and through symbols which belong to the life of the community to which he belongs, he seeks to express the vision of inner reality which he has seen. Thus true art is an interpretation of the universe. So-called art, which merely stirs the emotions and gives passing pleasure to the senses, but throws no light upon the wonder and the grandeur and the mystery of life, is not really worthy of the name. Art, as we suggested earlier, is concerned with inwardness, *telos*, significance : only so far as it is providing these for man, is it fulfilling its true function in human affairs.

II

In the life of primitive peoples the phenomenon which seems to correspond most closely to that of artistic activity is *shamanism*. There was indeed the dance-leader or master of song who seemed to be possessed with a spirit of frenzy and who succeeded in fashioning patterns of movement and sound with a skill which the ordinary tribesman did not possess : in his activities some kind of primitive artistry may be seen. Or there was the man who succeeded in drawing rough sketches of animals on cave-walls, and fashioned tiny amulets or charms : he, too, showed that he possessed powers denied to the ordinary man. But the *shaman* or medicine-man held a position of peculiar eminence in tribal life. He was believed to be in intimate touch with the spirits, and so to have knowledge far superior to that of ordinary mortals. Often he would fall into a trance or into a state of self-hypnosis and as a result would be able to reveal the secrets of the gods to his fellow-men. Though the office was partly hereditary

86

yet if a youth manifested such a disposition as marked him out as the possessor of the necessary gifts, he was trained to it and given the full rights and privileges pertaining thereto.

In lineal descent from these early *shamans* stand the soothsayers, seers and wise men and even many of the castes of priests and prophets of later days. Their task was to act as interpreters of life, unravelling its inner secrets, indicating what ought to be done in given circumstances and throwing light upon the future as far as they were able. An excellent example of the general outlook, as found in ancient Egypt, is provided by the story of Joseph which appears in the book of Genesis. When Pharaoh's butler and baker were assailed by dreams which seemed full of mystery, Joseph was able to give interpretations which were vindicated by later events. This in turn led to his being summoned to Pharaoh's aid when he, too, had dreams whose significance was hidden from him. What the magicians and wise men were unable to do, Joseph successfully accomplished and when the question arose as to who should be appointed viceroy over Egypt to organize plans against the coming famine, Pharaoh settled the matter by declaring, " Can we find such a one as this is, a man in whom the Spirit of God is ? " A similar thought occurs in a Babylonian context in the fifth chapter of the book of Daniel. Daniel, who had been set over the magicians, astrologers, Chaldeans and soothsayers because of his capacity to interpret dreams, is said by the queen to be a man in whom is the spirit of the holy gods. And " forasmuch as an excellent spirit and knowledge and understanding, interpreting of dreams and shewing of hard sentences and dissolving of doubts were found in the same Daniel" he was brought in before the king.

Thus in the ancient thought of mankind the men who seemed to possess outstanding gifts of insight and interpretation were believed to be inspired by unseen spirits and were treated with due honour and respect. What then are we to say of Hebrew thought in this regard? First and foremost we shall point to the phenomenon of Hebrew prophecy and say that these were the men who filled the role of the artist pre-eminently in the life of Israel. They were not, it is true, painters or sculptors, but they were poets and dramatists and it is possible that music was often employed in the service of their prophetic art. Above all they were men of the Spirit. It was through the Spirit that they were able to discern the meaning of contemporary events and to peer into the future. It was through the Spirit that they were able to paint their word-pictures and perform their dramatic acts. However deficient Hebrew social life may have been in the practice of other arts, there is nothing in the ancient world that can surpass the poetry of Jeremiah and the Psalmists and the vivid imagery of Ezekiel. These men certainly were artists if the function of the artist is to lay hold of the inner significance of events and express it in meaningful symbol.

To say this does not, of course, settle the question of the relationship between the great prophets of Israel and the ecstatics of earlier times. This is a question which has been much debated and it is hardly possible to give a final answer. It is clear that there were certain things in common between earlier and later prophecy and there are some who would claim that there was a straightforward development over the centuries, with the cruder phenomena of earlier times gradually being sloughed off. It may, however, equally well be argued that, whereas from first to last there was the groundwork of a natural phenomenon of which the art of today is a later manifestation, a new level of prophecy was established in and through the activity of those men who, by the help of the inner testimony of the Spirit of the Messiah, were able to bear witness to the sufferings of Christ and the glory that should follow. (1 *Pet.* 1 : 11). To *all* there was granted an insight into the inner meaning of reality, but to these chosen men there was revealed the secret of all history, the significance of the whole cosmic drama—the Christ, His sufferings and His glory.

Two other things may be said concerning this aspect of the Spirit's activity as shown forth in the Old Testament. As we have already suggested, there was little appreciation of the plastic arts among the Hebrews. Yet there are two important passages, one relating to the construction of the tabernacle and the other to the temple, where it becomes clear that this side of things was not altogether ignored. In *Exodus* 25–39 many chapters are devoted to the building and decorating of the tabernacle and to the designing of the priestly garments : these latter are said to have been " for glory and for beauty " and their construction was in the hands of those who were " filled with the spirit of wisdom ". Even more striking, however, are the words used in reference to the chief architect of the tabernacle and his assistant. " See, the Lord hath called by name Bezaleel . . . and he hath filled him with the spirit of God, in wisdom, in understanding, and in knowledge and in all manner of workmanship ; and he hath put in his heart that he may teach, both he and Aholiab. . . . Them hath he filled with wisdom of heart to work all manner of work, of the engraver and of the cunning workman, and of the embroiderer, in blue, and in purple, in scarlet, and fine linen, and of the weaver, even of them that do any work, and of those that devise cunning work " (*Ex.* 35 : 30–5). Similarly in regard to the temple it is said that David gave to Solomon his son " the pattern of all that he had by the spirit, of the courts of the house of the Lord, and of all the chambers round about " (1 *Chr.* 28 : 12).

Taking these two passages together with 2 *Chronicles* 3 and 4 and comparing them with the commentary of *Heb.* 8–10, we see that there is a distinct realization that a beautiful building and beautiful vestments can bear a real significance and that the designing of these objects depends in a very real way upon the inspiration of the divine Spirit. This means that the Bible is not without appreciation of artistic symbolism and Brother Every seems to be fully justified in writing thus on the subject of *Art and the Bible*. " The gist of the matter," he says, " is that there is ' a pattern in the mount' revealed to the craftsmen who are to rear up the Tabernacle and fashion its furniture." (He is referring to the Exodus chapters.) " They are not passive instruments; they themselves are filled with the spirit of God ' in wisdom and understanding and in all manner of workmanship'. But their designs are not wholly their own. They are impelled to translate into earthly ' types and shadows ' realities beyond the range of direct description. The whole of the Psalms and the prophets, the epistles of St. Paul and the Book of Revelation, seem to me to witness with singular consistency to the same idea of the function of symbols."[1] Through artistic symbolism the Spirit brings home the meaning and value of certain areas of experience to the hearts of men.

The other thing which may be pointed out is that in Israel's Wisdom Literature the Spirit was practically equated with Wisdom and various functions which in the earlier part of the Old Testament were assigned to the Spirit, came here to be attributed to the working of the divine Wisdom. The significance of this fact for our investigation lies in the support which it gives to our contention that in the thought of the Hebrews it was through the Spirit that gifts of creativity and special knowledge were bestowed upon men. " Privileged knowledge and understanding of God and of the divine purposes and achievements",[2] these are predicated of Wisdom and

[1] *Letter in Theology*, Dec. 43.
[2] A. J. Macdonald, *The Interpreter Spirit and Human Life*, p. 47.

so, by inference, of the Holy Spirit. It cannot be claimed
that there is any clear or consistent doctrine of the Spirit
in the Wisdom Literature, but at least there is the suggestion
that the Spirit is the inspirer of the creative insight whereby
life is evaluated at its true worth and its meaning made
plain.

III

In seeking to understand the New Testament approach
to this part of our subject let us begin with the striking
statement of *John* 1 : 14–18. " And the Word was made
flesh and dwelt (lit. ' tabernacled ') among us (and we
beheld his glory, the glory as of the only begotten of the
Father,) full of grace and truth. No man hath seen God
at any time ; the only begotten Son which is in the bosom
of the Father, he hath declared (lit. interpreted or exhibited)
him." Certain words in this statement take us back
immediately to the Old Testament. The ' tabernacling '
of the Word recalls the tabernacle of the Most High which
stood in the midst of the camp in the days of the desert
wanderings : the ' Glory ' recalls the Shekinah of the
God of Israel which ' filled the tabernacle ' (*Ex.* 40 : 34)
when the work of its construction was complete. Moreover we recall that when Moses was about to go up a
second time into the holy mount, to receive the tables
of stone, he asked : ' 'Show me, I pray thee, thy glory."
And the Lord replied : " Thou canst not see my face :
for man shall not see me and live." Over against this
background is set the amazing new fact : God has dwelt
in the very midst of His people in the person of the man
Christ Jesus : His glory rested upon him and indeed
filled him (though men did not always behold the glory) :
we who are Christian witnesses have seen his glory " the
glory such as the only Son receives from his Father "
(Archbishop Bernard's translation) : in short, the only-
begotten has interpreted the Father to man.

The whole of the Fourth Gospel may be regarded as an extended commentary upon these early claims. As we suggested in our discussion of the Old Testament, there is a strong assumption running through the Pentateuch that both the tabernacle and the Law were modelled according to a pattern designed by God Himself. Moses and his fellow-workers were granted, through the Spirit, a vision of heavenly realities and this enabled them to set before the people such an interpretation of Beauty and Truth as under the particular circumstances of the time they could apprehend. But in contrast to the earlier dispensation, there now stands One who replaces both *Torah* and Temple. He in His personal life is the very image of the invisible God : He, the only begotten Son, reveals the Father's love to men. And this revelation is the exhibition of God's glory, a glory which can be characterized as fullness of grace and truth.

What then do these two words mean ? In the Old Testament it is *mercy* and truth that are normally coupled together (*Ps.* 85 : 9, 10—a passage which may well have been in the writer's mind) but for some reason the author here prefers the Greek word ' *charis*,' although he does not use it outside the Prologue of his Gospel. No final reason can be given for this preference, though it may be suggested that the word *charis* would more easily convey, to one familiar with the Greek language, the thought of outward graciousness, loveliness or charm. The author is clearly concerned with that which was manifested outwardly through the personal life of the Logos and we may therefore infer that graciousness, rather than compassion, was the thought which he wished more particularly to emphasize. This more Hellenistic note in regard to *charis* is confirmed by the fact that in this Gospel, as Dr. W. F. Howard points out (*Christianity according to St. John.* p. 184), *Aletheia* (Truth) is used in its characteristically Greek sense and bears little trace of the original Hebrew connotation. It stands for ' reality ' as contrasted with phantasy. " The self-communicating divine life has actually come to men in Jesus Christ . . . Truth is not a correct conception of God to be apprehended by the intellect so much as a revelation of reality to be received in a personal relationship."[1]

Thus the claim of these pregnant words becomes clear. In Jesus Christ there shines forth a glory which reveals the Beauty and the Truth of God Himself. It is not a beauty and a truth contained within the body which performed actions and the mind which produced words. These in themselves were not the means of exhibiting eternal realities. Rather it was the life lived in the constant relationship of beloved Son to Father which interpreted the Father to men. Men could truly behold the beauty and the reality of the divine life only as they themselves entered into relationship with Him who was Himself in relationship with the Father. For in the last resort ' the flesh ', however beautiful it might be, could profit nothing ; even the words, however true, could not cause men to apprehend reality. But in relationship, in the Spirit (*John* 6 : 63), Beauty and Truth were exhibited, Beauty and Truth could be received, and thus the Glory of God could dwell amongst men and they be transformed into His Image. To " as many as received Him, to them gave He the right to become the sons of God " (*John* 1 : 12).

This general thought appears again in the Paraclete Passages which form so notable a part of the discourses in the Upper Room. Many attempts have been made to determine the precise meaning of the Greek word *parakletos*. In general it stands for advocate or helper and in the history of religion it or its equivalent may represent ' spokesman', ' intercessor', 'mediator 'or ' representative '.[2]

Yet within the particular context of this Gospel the

[1] *Ib.*, pp. 185–6.
[2] See article in *Review of Religion*, March 1943, pp. 284 ff.

meaning which seems far the most apt is guide or interpreter. During His incarnate life Jesus had acted as His disciples' guide : He had initiated them into the mystery of His Kingdom and had guided them into a growing knowledge of its demands and privileges. Now on the eve of His departure He promises that the Spirit will come who will lead them into all the Truth. In other words, He will continue the work of interpreting to them the revelation of ultimate reality as it is found in Christ Himself. Just as Christ in the Spirit had interpreted the Father, so will the Spirit interpret Christ to the disciples and through the glory revealed in them will in turn lead others to believe in Christ. "As Jesus has in all His words and works glorified His Father, that is, has revealed His inmost nature and character, so will the Spirit bring to light all the grace and truth which their imperfectly trained vision has prevented the disciples from discerning in Him from whom the Father has withheld no treasure in the unsearchable riches of His love."[1]

It remains to refer briefly to St. Paul's teaching which, especially in the *Second Epistle to the Corinthians*, is closely parallel to that of the Fourth Gospel. The key chapter is the third. Here again it is essential to pay attention to the Old Testament background in seeking to interpret St. Paul's thought. Actually he is drawing a sharp contrast between the two dispensations—the Old Covenant which centred in a written law and the New Covenant which belongs to the realm of Spirit. The written law, he says, kills, whereas the Spirit makes alive. Yet in spite of its stern and unbending character, the law was surrounded by a certain *aura* of ' glory '. It had a temporary mission to fulfil in revealing the righteousness which does belong to the inner constitution of the universe. So, St. Paul argues, " if the administration of death, which was engraved in letters of stone, was invested with glory—so much so,

[1] Howard, *op. cit.*, p. 77.

that the children of Israel could not gaze at the face of Moses on account of the dazzling glory that was fading from his face ; surely the administration of the Spirit must be invested with still greater glory " (*Moffatt*).

But, he goes on, Moses was forced to hang a veil over his face to prevent the children of Israel from seeing that the glory was fading away and in a figurative sense, that veil still separates them from the vision of God's true glory. Only by turning to the Lord can the veil be removed (St. Paul here draws upon *Ex.* 34 : 34). But ' the Lord ' must be interpreted as meaning the Spirit, for it is those who turn to the new dispensation of the Spirit who find themselves enjoying perfect freedom. So, he concludes, we all with face unveiled can gaze upon the glory of the Lord (which as he will show in 4 : 6 is focused in the face of Jesus Christ) and be transformed into the same image by the agency of the Lord the Spirit.

There are difficulties of interpretation in this passage but the general sense seems clear. The central thought is that of ' glory', which, as Dr. R. H. Strachan suggests, is to him just " a radiant self-expression " of the divine, (*Moffatt Commentary on 2 Cor.*, p. 86). The glory of God has been once for all revealed in the ' face ' of Jesus Christ. That face possesses and expresses and interprets the very character of God, and brings it into living relation with men. All that remains for man to do is to gaze upon that glory. So he gradually reflects the glory as in a mirror, becomes related to the glory, becomes transformed into an image of the glory—all through the operation of the Spirit, part of whose activity it is to reproduce the glory of God in the life of man. In brief, the Spirit of God is the Divine artist. In the face of Jesus Christ and in the faces of His followers, He paints a living picture of the eternal glory of God.

As we seek to summarize the results of our enquiry in this chapter, we shall turn again to the dialectic of Creation and Redemption to which we have already referred. In the first place it seems impossible to make sense of the world unless we can assume that in the divine act of Creation the values of truth and beauty were in some way woven into the very fabric of the universe, and man himself was endowed with faculties to understand and appreciate them. The day has passed for arguing about objectivity and subjectivity in this connection. It is enough to believe that God has created man in relation to his universe and that within this relationship the values of truth and beauty are firmly established.

This is not to say, however, that man immediately recognizes these values. All life, in fact, is in the nature of an education towards such a recognition. And in this education man is dependent upon those who have learned before him, or upon those creative men, who, belonging to his own circle, are yet able to pierce through to the inner significance of life in a way which he finds it impossible to do himself. It is these latter whom we designate creative artists.

Now it is an interesting fact that artists themselves are the first to recognize that in this work of possessing and interpreting some aspect of reality, they are dependent upon something which they call ‘ Inspiration’. (And we may remind ourselves that ‘ inspiration ’ literally means the inbreathing of spirit.) Thus Mr. J. B. Priestley has an interesting passage in his book *Rain upon God's hill* in which he asks how this ‘ inspiration ’ comes to man. “ I believe,” he says, “ that during those few hours of effortless but extremely rewarding creation, I was able without being then aware of it, to tap a reservoir of creative energy and skill, which reservoir is really the source of all so-called inspiration. Do not mistake me here. I am not claiming that a play of mine was really the work of some world-mind. The play itself, the people and scenes in it, all these are coloured and shaped by my own ego and exhibit all my own particular weaknesses and merits. But that triumphant rush of energy and skill enabling me to run across the dramatic tightwire effortlessly, just for this one act, was not really my own doing and owed its existence to the fact which might or might not be the product of chance that this immensely greater mind could for the time being sustain my own mind. I was indeed not so much a creator myself as an instrument of creation."

Again, in his essay in *The Intent of the Artist*, Roger Sessions discusses the same phenomenon. The first stage in the composer's work, he says, is what is generally known as 'inspiration'. It may come in a flash or it may grow and develop gradually. "Inspiration is the impulse which sets creation in movement, it is also the energy which keeps it going. The composer's principal problem is that of recapturing it in every phase of his work ; of bringing, in other words, the requisite amount of energy to bear on every detail as well as constantly on his vision of the whole" (pp. 126–7).

Surely we may claim that this dimly recognized impulse, which makes possible the beginning of a creative interpretation, is the work of the Spirit Himself. Man needs, indeed, to place himself in a real relation with the sights or sounds by which he is surrounded, but then this more than ordinary thing happens—man is laid hold of by the Spirit and enabled to set forth in symbol the meaning of what he sees or hears. Thus there is an Art of Creation which may truly be regarded as due to the activity of the Spirit.

But such artistic expressions can never be allowed to remain as ends in themselves. Final meaning cannot be captured within a static form. Always there must be dynamic action, a movement towards that final *Telos* which God has designed. Yet man longs to remain within the enjoyment of the present beauty or truth. He clings to what he has already seen or achieved. So his creation becomes an end in itself—a final representation of reality as he imagines—an idol before which he is prepared to bow down and worship, serving himself in its service. This is the peril of a false aestheticism and a static intellectualism. " The aesthete is no more released from his own desires than the practical man and he is without the practical man's healthy outlet in action. He sees life, not indeed in relation to action, but to his own personal sensation. . . . He tries to make his whole attitude artistic —that is, contemplative. He is always looking and prying and savouring, *savourant*, as he would say, when he ought to be living. The result is that there is nothing to *savourer*. All art springs . . . out of keen emotion towards life, and even the power to appreciate art needs this emotional reality in the spectator. The aesthete leads at best a parasite-artistic life, dogged always by death and corruption."[1] A similar judgment might be passed on the pure intellectual who weaves his web again and again around discovered truth. Through man's self-interest and failure in these respects, beauty and truth are prostituted and Creation spoiled.

As in other realms of life, then, the work of the Spirit in the Redemption of Art is always necessary. For however we may theorize about its cause, the fact of tragedy and corruption in nature is indisputable, and the task of the artist is to become the instrument of the Spirit for the Redemption of Nature by bringing new meaning into view. As Paul Tillich so aptly remarks : " A great picture or statue is an anticipation of the new earth, a revelation of the mystery of nature. It is a piece of stone or plant transformed into a bearer of spiritual meaning. It is nature

[1] J. E. Harrison, *Ancient Art and Ritual*, pp. 214-15.

elevated above itself, showing its tragedy and, at the same time, its victory over its tragedy."[1] Especially is this true in such an age as that in which we live. " In a tormented age, art has to transform the obsessive ugliness, not to offer a mirage of pleasure to suffering men. If art fails to solve their suffering, men instinctively turn away from a deep and insoluble experience to simple dope. Jazz and swing music are the typical expression of unsolved unhappiness."[2]

This all leads us to that central and final interpretation of the world's tragedy—the Cross of Calvary. Not that the Cross in itself could have been the interpretation. The disciples were bewildered and despairing. The grim tragedy stared them in the face. The apparent weakness of God was overwhelmed by the cruel strength of man. The light which had begun to shine into their world was blotted out, and darkness reigned.

Yet did it not behove the Christ thus to suffer and enter into His Glory ? Was there not a Paraclete who would glorify Him by revealing to waiting hearts the meaning of the things which had come to pass (*John* 16 : 13)? The whole of the New Testament is witness to the fact that, through the activity of the Spirit, meaning came into a shattered world, and that men found in the Cross the final symbol of the possession of Eternal Life. The glory of the latter house became greater than that of the former (*Hag.* 2 : 9). Through the Spirit the many are brought out of corruption into the liberty of the glory of the sons of God (*Rom.* 8 : 31).

This great Biblical truth has been expressed so forcefully and so beautifully by Dr. L. S. Thornton that we shall conclude this chapter by quoting his words : " Calvary," he writes, " was interpreted in the light of Pentecost. The two events were mutually dependent. When the Spirit was given, then their (i.e. the disciples') minds were illuminated

---

[1] *Christendom : Summer*, 1945, p. 305.
[2] Kathleen Raine in *Our Changing World*, p. 207.

with the full truth of God's love in Christ. Pentecost presupposed Calvary, and could have had no distinctive meaning without Calvary. Yet the meaning of Calvary became accessible only through the outpouring of the Spirit at Pentecost.

Pentecost brought an illumination of the mind which transformed their outlook. Everything looked different, as everything looks different when a drought is followed by a shower of rain. The very rays of the sun seem different in such circumstances. The rays which were scorching are now pleasantly warming. All the details of nature are the same ; yet all have been transformed. So it was after Pentecost. The souls of the disciples were like watered gardens. With the descending streams of the Spirit came the revelation of God's love. The truth for which their souls thirsted now refreshed them. In them were fulfilled these words from the Psalter :

Thy loving kindness O Lord, is in the heavens. . . .
How precious is Thy loving kindness O God ! . . .
They shall be watered with the fatness of thy house ;
And thou shall make them drink of the river of thy
    pleasures.
For with thee is the fountain of life :
In thy light shall we see light."[1]

Truly the light of the knowledge of the glory of God has shone forth in the face of Jesus Christ : and we all, with faces unveiled, can behold that glory and reflect that glory until we are transfigured into the same image by the direct agency of the Spirit of the Lord.

[1] *Op. cit.*, 104.

VENI, SANCTE SPIRITUS

> "The vital point in our knowledge of the Gospel
> lies in our answer to the question: 'How is the
> Holy Spirit given'?"
>
> Quoted by Dr. H. Wheeler Robinson.

> "At one point of nature and history, and only at one
> point, faith hears the unequivocal and everlasting *Yea*
> of God. God has spoken His Yea in His Son and His
> Spirit keeps prompting us, with all the means that
> heaven can use, to utter our *Amen*."
>
> *Christ and the World of Thought*, Daniel Lamont.

WE COME at length to the focal point of our whole
enquiry. We have discussed the nature of spirit, and
have outlined the Biblical account of the revelation of
Holy Spirit. Proceeding further, we have examined four
different areas of human life and activity, and have suggested
that the activity of the Spirit may be described in terms
taken from each of these various fields. When a necessity
arises for bearing witness to that which is from the beyond,
no human language can be final. Yet we *must* speak and
can speak if we remain faithful to the great Biblical categories
which are themselves derived from the archetypal experiences common to all mankind.

This brings us, however, to certain final and all-important
questions. Assuming that the Holy Spirit is still active
in the world today, is there anything that men can do to
prepare the way for His activities in human life? Above
all, is there a way whereby man can receive the Holy
Spirit and enjoy His abiding presence in his own heart?
These are vital questions which cannot be brushed aside
or ignored. Lincoln Bible Institute

It is of little use to describe the activities of the Spirit in former ages, if it is impossible to believe that He operates in the same way today. It is a counsel of despair to suggest to men that God is at work through His Spirit, but that there is no means whatsoever of coming into contact with the Spirit and receiving the benefits of His activity into life and experience. We shall seek, then, in this chapter to draw out the more practical consequences of the conclusions to which we have already been led.

I

Let us begin by glancing at the records of the preludes to the new activity of the Spirit which are to be found in the early chapters of the Gospels and of the *Acts of the Apostles*. John heralded the coming of one who would baptize " with the Holy Ghost and with fire" (*Luke* 3 : 16). He looked for the inauguration of a new era in which the powers of heaven would be manifested in the world and moral evils would be swept away. To prepare for this great event, he sternly summoned men to *repent*. So when Jesus began His public ministry, He also proclaimed the Kingdom of God, and called upon men to *repent* and believe the good news. And once more, when, on the day of Pentecost, the people were pricked in their heart and cried out anxiously to know what they must do, the answer was still ' *Repent*.' In other words, before there can be an entrance into the new order, and an experience of the powers of the age to come, there must necessarily be a *repentance* with all that the word implies.

What, then, does the word ' repent ' mean in its New Testament context ? Modern research has made it abundantly clear that the idea of sorrow for sin is certainly not primary, and need not be involved at all. Rather the emphasis lies on a complete change of attitude, a turning away from one manner of life and outlook and the adoption of another : in particular in the New Testament there is always the thought of turning back to God, of recognizing His sovereign rule, and of casting oneself in utter dependence upon Him. But one further thing needs to be said. Repentance must always be interpreted in relation to the background of accepted standards and ideas against which it is set. Thus in the Old Testament we find it being set over against a generally accepted system of idol-worship, or in contrast to a formal sacrificial system, or in opposition to a debased standard of social practices. The historical experience of any people seems to include periods when the general thought and outlook is rigidly set in a particular direction and, especially in the life of Israel, it was the task of the prophets to challenge generally accepted ideas in such periods, and to recall people to their dependence upon the living God and to their responsibility towards Him.

There can be little doubt that within the period immediately preceding the Christian era one type of thought had won wider and wider acceptance amongst the Jewish people. It was the type which we should call legalism. To adhere to a set of rigidly prescribed rules of conduct became the be-all and end-all of life. Some might regard their duties and responsibilities more seriously than others, some might acknowledge a more elaborate system than others, but in the general thought of the people a recognition of the Law, and a sustained attempt to obey its regulations, constituted the whole duty of man. And it is within this context that the call to repentance, especially in the preaching of Jesus and His apostles, has to be set. It was a call to turn away from the bondage of the Law to the freedom of the living Spirit of God, a call to abandon the assumption that the world was an enclosed system of Law into which no other principle could enter, and to believe that God was continually acting by His Spirit freely and powerfully to the redemption and salvation of mankind, a call to withdraw from a world in which devotion to regulation was the dominant motive, and to enter a world in which a relation to God through His Spirit could be the controlling factor in life. If it be felt that the one word ' Repent ' is incapable of bearing so full a meaning, we can at least see that this was the central challenge of the Christian faith by observing the reactions of leading Pharisees who came into contact with Jesus and His gospel. Nothing is more prominent in the writings of St. Paul than the vivid contrast between life under the Law and life according to to the Spirit : and in the story of Nicodemus, the altogether novel idea which this master of Israel found himself utterly unable to grasp, was that there could be another order coming down from above and breaking into his well-regulated world, an order of freedom and Spirit and regenerating activity which could initiate him into the secret of eternal life.

Thus, according to the New Testament, the indispensable preliminary to any new life in the Spirit is a change of outlook—may we say a change of imagination ?—a change from a system of thought and outlook which is bounded by the laws and possibilities of *this* world and a glad recognition of a personal living Spirit who, proceeding out of *that* world, manifests the laws and the possibilities of *that* world, in the very midst of this world which is so familiar to us. We have dwelt on this point at some length because of our conviction that without this preliminary change, all other talk to our own day and generation about receiving the Spirit is bound to be in vain. For we are living in an age which has its own standards and outlook. In a word, it is the Age of Science. Since the rise of experimental science, one department after another of human activity has fallen under its control, one after another of its achievements has captured the human imagination, until today it has come to be generally assumed that there is nothing in the universe which is beyond the power of the scientist to know and ultimately to control. To obey the laws of the scientific universe and to enjoy its benefits has become the chief end of man.

Now just as the legalism of the Pharisees was not "all wrong", so we are not for a moment suggesting that the system of the scientists is wholly perverse. But what was the desperate quality of the Pharisees' system was its imagined *finality*. They were tireless in their search after ' righteousness ', but even this ' righteousness ' was contained within their own system. And Jesus cried that unless the righteousness of His disciples should *exceed* (*i.e.* transcend) that of the Pharisees, they could not hope to enter into the world of higher reality which is the Kingdom of God. So with the scientist. He is tireless in his search for ' truth ', but again it is ' truth ' which is contained within his own system. He insists, in other words, that ' truth ' which cannot be apprehended by scientific methods has no real claim to the name but belongs to the realm of phantasy or wishful thinking. And surely Jesus would have cried to this generation that unless our ' truth ' exceeds or transcends that of the scientist, we cannot hope to see the vision of those higher realities which belong to the Kingdom of God.

To some, the above may seem a caricature of the careful and self-effacing work of hosts of modern scientists, just as to some, Jesus' criticism of the Pharisees seems unjustified in view of the pious and unselfish lives which many of them led. But what we are concerned with, as we believe He was concerned with, is a system of thought which gradually establishes itself and comes to exert a kind of magnetic influence upon the attitudes and outlooks of ordinary people. It was the rigid finality and the this-worldliness of the Pharisaic system which Jesus condemned, for its effect had been to cause the ordinary man to believe that through living within a system of rules he could attain all that life could offer : so it is the all-inclusive claims and the materialism of the scientists' system which we venture to condemn, for again its effect has been to cause the ordinary man to believe that natural forces are everything, and that his life can consist only in being borne along on the tide of evolution, accepting the benefits which the controlled powers of nature can offer him, and waiting for the day when those which are at present uncontrolled will also be harnessed to his service. Such an outlook is so foreign to that of Jesus and His apostles, that unless there be a radical change, there seems little prospect of the doctrine of the Spirit regaining any relevance. We are called upon therefore to repent, to turn away, that is, from all closed systems and false philosophies which leave no place for the Living God, to turn to Him Who made the universe, and controls the universe, and still acts within it by His life-giving Spirit : and turning thus, the veil is taken away from our eyes, and we begin to know the liberty of that same Spirit and to experience the reality of that other world which is the world of eternal life.

II

If now the initial change has been made, and we are prepared to recognize that the activity of God can truly be manifested within our world by His Spirit, what is the next stage ? The next stage, we suggest, is the whole-hearted acceptance of the principle that only through relationship or relatedness can the Spirit operate within our own individual lives and within those of the community. The Spirit does not operate *in vacuo* : there must be a true relationship with the *natural* order so that we may experience the *creative* activities of the Spirit; there must be a true relationship with the *saved* order so that we may experience the *redemptive* activities of the Spirit. We shall briefly consider each in turn.

(*a*) So far as the natural order is concerned, it is becoming increasingly evident that unless man will seek to understand and co-operate with his natural environment, he cannot escape ultimate disaster. He must learn the laws of fertility and obey them : if he seeks simply to exploit nature for his own immediate profits he will finally starve. So, too, he must learn the laws governing power, and its control : if the vast forces of nature are not handled with constant precautions and unceasing care, they will overwhelm him in devastation and ruin. Further he must learn to order his community life in such a way as to avoid the blight of unemployment and the explosive forces of revolution. Such an experiment as has been made in the Tennessee Valley provides an outstanding example of the way in which man can seek to co-operate with all the natural forces in his environment—with the river and the land, the forest and the soil, the mines and the farms, technical resources and economic laws, social amenities and facilities for cultural development : when man sets himself deliberately to enter into a true and living relationship with the whole environment, learning humbly, experimenting patiently, acting vigorously, then there comes into being a real harmony of the Spirit, a partial and temporary manifestation of that order which the Creator-Spirit is at all times seeking to establish.

Thus we believe that it is possible for man to enjoy a true experience of the Spirit's power and inspiration through his relationship with the natural order : in his relationship with Life, with Power, with Order, with Beauty, he is moved by a Spirit beyond his own, and can recognize, if he will, that the hand of the Lord has been laid upon him. But as we have discovered in our enquiry, man is constantly doing despite to that Spirit Whom he meets in these relationships. He seeks to make that with which he holds relationship, Absolute. He feeds upon life like a parasite : he lusts after power ; he makes Law his god : he idealizes Nature and seeks to luxuriate in her beauty. So the gifts of the Spirit in relationship are corrupted by man's self-centredness. Ever desiring to possess, he becomes possessed, not by the Spirit, but by demons who drive him forward to his doom. Unless there be another order breaking in to save and redeem him, the relationship in the Spirit will be marred beyond repair. But this is the claim of the Christian faith; it is indeed the claim of the whole Bible—that there is an order of Redemption in which God *through His Word* calls man into relationship with Himself, and that that relationship becomes established *through the Spirit*.

(*b*) The great principle of the redeemed order is that man now receives the Spirit through his relationship with a personal Word rather than with a natural environment. The Word of God comes to a man—to Abraham, to Moses, to Jeremiah : it is a Word of challenge, for it calls man away from his idolatry of the natural order, it is a Word of promise, for it tells of the new heaven and the new earth wherein dwelleth righteousness. It is a Word from the other world and yet it must be expressed in the language of this world. But the most powerful language of this world is the pattern of a human life. So the God who at sundry times and in divers manners spake through the prophets, at the last spoke through his Son. There the Word came to a focus and final expression, and it is as man enters into relationship with Him that the Spirit can operate effectively and dynamically to the complete transformation of heart and life. For as it has been said, " It is the setting of the mind on Christ in the revelation of His graciousness and of the infinite love of God in it, that makes it possible for the Spirit of Christ to act unto the soul's complete deliverance."

III

Relationship with the living Word of God is, then, the all-important condition for the receiving of the Spirit. But ' relationship ' is an abstract and colourless term.

May we not seek, by turning back again to the natural order, to find metaphors and images which will more vividly bring home to our imaginations this great fact with which we are concerned? We shall attempt to do this by considering in turn the four aspects of the Spirit's activity already described in the central chapters of the book.

(1) *Christ the Word of Life.* This is, in a peculiar way, the emphasis of the Fourth Gospel. "In Him was life." "The water that I shall give him shall be in him a well of water springing up into everlasting life." "I am the Bread of Life." "He that followeth me shall not walk in darkness but shall have the light of life." There is hardly anything which man needs for his natural well-being—air, food, water, light—which is not used as a metaphor either for the Word Himself or for the gift of the Spirit which He bestows. He who comes to Jesus (one word describing relationship) will never be hungry, he who believes on Jesus (another word describing relationship) will never thirst.

If now we are to think of Christ as the source of all life, we are justified in using physical terms to suggest the way in which the relationship can be established. Thus the Bible does not hesitate to speak of the beginning of the process as a birth from above. "Except a man be born of water and of the Spirit he cannot enter into the Kingdom of God." "The wind (*pneuma*) bloweth where it listeth and thou hearest the sound thereof but canst not tell whence it cometh and whither it goeth: so is every one that is born of the Spirit" (*pneuma*). Just as the coming of water makes new life to spring out of the earth: just as the coming of the breeze makes new energy to stir where hitherto there has been lassitude and lifelessness: so the coming of the Spirit brings to birth new life, new hope, new power, a new relationship— "a well of water springing up into everlasting life." Moreover the continuance of the process is referred to as "eating the flesh of the Son of Man and drinking His blood" (*John* 6 : 53). "Just as the living Father sent me and I live by the Father, so he who feeds on me will also live by me" (*John* 6 : 37, *Moffatt*). Here the language of metabolism is freely used. It is only by eating, drinking and breathing that any living organism can avoid decay. In fact it must continually be sucking suitable food from its environment or it will inevitably wither and die.[1] So it is in the life of the redeemed order. Both the individual and the community can only retain their vitality in so far as they are continually drawing their sustenance from their appropriate environment. But this environment is not physical but personal. There must be the constant feeding upon the loaf which is Christ, drinking at the well which is Christ, breathing from the source of pure air which is Christ : and the food is the Spirit, the water is the Spirit, the breath is the Spirit. "It is the Spirit which giveth life : the flesh profiteth nothing."

This language naturally leads us to think of the Sacraments and their place in the life of the Spirit. In a certain sense every gift provided for us within the natural order which sustains and enriches our lives, may be regarded as a sacrament by which the Spirit can operate effectively within us. The very processes of metabolism can be sacramental channels for the Spirit's gift of natural life. How much more can those special Sacraments of the Gospel, which are designed to bring vividly before our imaginations the generating and sustaining activities of Christ Himself, prove to be means by which His Spirit can operate effectively to the establishing and strengthening of that life which is eternal ? Thus the participation in a ritual of hallowed water, the eating of bread and drinking of wine which have been consecrated through the Word, can be sacramental channels for the receiving of life in

[1] Cp. Schrodinger, *op. cit.*, pp. 71-2.

the Spirit. To say this is not to bind the activity of the Spirit within a particular system of formal observances, but rather to bear witness to the Spirit's use of material means upon which we sought to lay emphasis at the very beginning of our study.

(2) *Christ the Power of God* (1 *Cor.* 1 : 24). This is in a peculiar way the emphasis of St. Mark's Gospel though it also appears prominently in the writings of St. Paul. From the very beginning of the Marcan testimony there is reference to the dynamic power which Jesus exercised. In His dealings with the demon-possessed and those afflicted with divers diseases, He manifested such a power as to astonish His contemporaries. " What is this ? " they asked. " With authority He commandeth the unclean spirits and they obey Him." But His power was not to be reserved for Himself alone. Having chosen His twelve apostles He gave them power also to heal sicknesses and to cast out devils (3 : 15). In relationship with Him they became strong : out of relationship with Him, their power vanished away (*Matt.* 17 : 20).

If then we think of Christ as the source of every form of power needed for the challenge of life, we may again use images taken from the physical world to describe how man may draw upon this power for his daily needs. There is a notable portrayal of this aspect of the spiritual life in Dr. R. W. Dale's Lectures on *The Atonement* and we cannot do better than quote at length a passage which is vivid in its imagery and entirely apposite to our subject. " The Christian man," he writes, " does not simply develop and perfect his own life ; he is constantly receiving and appropriating the life and power of the Son of God. . . . Our relation to Christ is absolutely unique. And yet, perhaps, some imperfect symbol of it may be found in our relation to the material universe. Man is a free person- ality, encompassed by a system of forces which transcend all the measures of his science. To these forces, which we now learn are perhaps but various forms of one great Force which remains constant from age to age, man is mysteriously related and from moment to moment he is dependent on them. In every thought, however light and wayward, that passes through his intellect; in every emotion, however transient, which ripples across the surface of his normal life; in every volition; there is some expenditure of that part of this universal energy which has been accumulated in the nerves and tissues of his physical organisation. Whatever power belongs to man comes to him from the appropriation of force from without. . . . The history of the material progress of the race is the history of the growing power of man, arising from the gradual extension of his alliances with the forces which surround him. His proudest achievements are their work rather than his. He arms himself with the strength of the winds and the tides. He liberates the latent energy which has been condensed and treasured up in coal, transforms it into heat, generates steam, and sweeps across a continent without weariness and with the swiftness of a bird. He makes the electric fluid his messenger, and it carries his words under the ocean to remote shores. Moving freely among the stupendous energies by which he is encompassed, he is strong in their strength, and they give to his volitions, powerless apart from them—a large and effective expression.

" The history of man's triumphs in the province of his higher and spiritual life is also the history of the gradual extension of his alliance with a Force which is not his own. There is no proportion between the native strength of his will and the perfection which he achieves through Christ. Every good work is a manifestation of the Divine power, in which alone we can be strong. . . . In the spiritual, as in the material sphere, man is a free personality surrounded by a vast and unmeasurable Power which is not his own, but through which his history may become bright with the glory of the noblest achievements. In Christ we are 'made partakers of the divine nature.' "[1]

Much might have been added to this statement in the light of more modern scientific development and yet Dr. Dale's chief emphasis needs no alteration. Just as man seeks to relate himself to the powers and energies resident in the physical universe, so he should seek to relate himself to the Power of Christ which belongs to his spiritual universe. Men will spend days, months, even years, in an unwearied search for ways and means of utilizing more of the vast physical energy which the universe contains : by experiment, by co-operative enterprises, by patient observation, they seek to receive that power which they believe is available for those who can discover the laws of its disposal. How much more should the Christian man devote himself to such active commerce with Christ Himself, to such a constant discontent with his own powers and achievements and to such a yearning for new energies to manifest themselves in the very midst of his own imperfections and failures, that more and more he may be strengthened with might by the Spirit of Christ in his inner man and may expand and grow into the utilization of all the resources of God !

(3) *Christ the Lord.* It is from a relationship with Christ as Lord that all possibilities of order within the Christian community are derived. This is in a peculiar way the emphasis of St. Paul in the New Testament. In the key-passage of *Philippians* 2, the result of the self-humiliation and sacrificial obedience of Christ Jesus is set forth in glowing terms as an exaltation to a place of supreme authority from which He is able to exercise Lordship over all those who dwell in heaven and earth and even under the earth. In the great credal affirmation of 1 *Cor.* 8 : 6 over against all so-called ' lords ' of this world, Christ Jesus is acknowledged as the one supreme Lord, " by

[1] Fifth Edition, pp. 412–17. *Congregational Union Lecture*, 1875.

whom are all things and we by Him". Submission to Him, loyalty to Him, are essential requirements for a genuinely Christian community : at the same time the community is knit together and cemented in its fellowship by standing under the protection and guidance and authority of the common Lord.

How then is this related to the receiving of the Holy Spirit ? The answer surely is to be found in 1 *Corinthians* 12 : 3. When a man openly confesses that Jesus is the Lord, it becomes unmistakably evident that the Holy Spirit is actively present in his heart. In other words, the Holy Spirit operates within relationship. As the individual enters into relationship with the one Lord he finds himself caught up into a new experience of fellowship which is none other than the *koinonia* of the Holy Ghost. Thus, in and through every occasion on which the individual or the community expresses loyalty and fealty to the one Lord in word or in deed, the Holy Spirit operates powerfully and in very truth it may be said that the Holy Spirit has been received.

As I write the memory comes to me of a conversation with one who had recently been spending a holiday in the midst of the Welsh mountains. I enquired of him whether he had enjoyed the experience, but received a somewhat surprising reply. " Not altogether," he said. " They have the effect of putting you too firmly in your proper place." The vision of grandeur and immensity had re-awakened a true sense of perspective which was not exactly congenial to a man's sense of his own stature and importance ! So the New Testament vision of exaltation and splendour which is contained in the title ' Lord ' never makes an immediate appeal to the natural man. Yet only through a true sense of proportion can community relations begin to develop. It is only when men bow in humility and reverence before an exalted Lord that they become fit to associate with one another on a basis of equality and respect. In short, when they cease from concentrating their attention upon their own rights and privileges and personal advantages and give themselves up to a contemplation of the glory of the Lord Christ and of the way in which all are on the same level in the service of His Kingdom, then the foundations of true community are being well and truly laid and the Spirit is operating to the production of a really harmonious fellowship.

Herein lies the importance of services of public prayer and worship. They are occasions for the re-gaining of true perspective in relation to Christ and to one another. A disciplined life of devotion may prove to be an effective instrument for the reception of the Holy Spirit if it be kept free from the corrosions of legalism and formalism which so easily gather around it. The same is true of acts of witness and service. If done in obedience to the Lord Christ, they become expressions of loyalty to Him and thereby means of receiving His Spirit. For wherever relation is truly realized there the Spirit acts with living power.

We may well conclude this section by quoting a paragraph from the last chapter of Canon C. E. Raven's book, *The Gospel and the Church*, in which he grapples with the question of how the community-pattern of the Apostolic age can be reproduced in the life of the Church today. "How," he asks, "is community, the *koinonia* of the Holy Spirit, to be attained? The answer to such a question is not difficult to state, however hard it may be to follow. Three conditions have to be fulfilled. First, the members must be individually dominated and integrated by a common loyalty, such as Christ can evoke and sustain; secondly, they must have the will and the means to express that loyalty in action, in the service of His world-wide commission; finally, they must be united as persons by mutual trust, sympathy and friendship, by the agape which binds them into an organic whole. Given these conditions the fellowship exercises a creative power vastly beyond what the members separately can attain. The inter-play of the individuals, far from distracting, enriches the energy of the whole. Results are achieved for which no one of them can claim credit, and which transcend the expectation and imagination of any. They can be, as St. Paul declared and the mystics have dreamed, to the Spirit of God what his hands and feet are to a man."[1]

(4) *Christ the Image of God*. This finally is the characteristic emphasis of the Epistle to the Hebrews, though it attains an almost equal prominence in the Pauline and Johannine writings. Christ is the effulgence of God's glory and the express image of His Person (*Heb.* 1 : 3). He is the image of the invisible God (*Col.* 1 : 15). He is the ' exegesis ' of the Father (*John* 1 : 18). And it is through relationship with Him that Christians become transformed into the same image by the Spirit of God.

What then does relationship involve within this area of thought and experience ? Clearly we are here concerned with the language and metaphors of the creative artist. For him, the matter of supreme importance is that he should be able to yield himself up with complete *abandon* to the particular object or objects which he desires to represent in his work of art. He endeavours to live with the object, to contemplate it, to wait upon it, to allow it to enter into the very fibre of his being, until the image of the object begins to take shape in his imagination and he finds himself able to express it through outward forms. If we may appeal once again to *The Intent of the Artist* we find this aspect of things admirably described both for the artist himself and also for those who seek to appreciate his work. " Works of art," we are told, " are worlds, complete, self-contained and different from our own, worlds to enter into and to live in. Just as the artist

[1] Raven, *The Gospel and The Church*, pp. 249–50.

has surrendered himself to the reality of his creation, so must we, the spectators, entirely yield to its strangeness. The work of art is not meant to be a corroboration of our actual sense of experience, but an expansion of it and also a liberation, a sudden disclosure of new perspectives in human existence. The spectator must enter into the work of art if a true æsthetic experience is to take place" (pp. 32-3).

How closely this language corresponds both to that of our Lord as recorded in the Fourth Gospel and to that of St. Paul in 2 *Corinthians* 3 ! " Abide in me," said our Lord, " and I in you." In fact, one of the characteristic words of the Fourth Gospel is ' abide '. There is in it a certain air of leisureliness combined with a challenge to intense activity. There must be the surrender to Him, the companying with Him, the waiting upon Him : at the same time there must be an intensity of apprehension, an urgency of desire to lay hold upon Him in every part of His being. To abide in Him is to enter into and live in the world which He, the image of God, represents. As this takes place, the Spirit operates within the relationship and produces an ever closer conformity with the image of the Christ, whom He is commissioned to glorify. St. Paul's thought in 2 *Cor.* 3 is exactly similar. The glory of God is revealed in the face of Jesus Christ, and that face must become the object of intense contemplation of all those who would experience the glory of God in their own lives. But as they yield themselves up to the vision, says St. Paul, as they enter into relationship with Him who is the image of God, the Spirit begins to operate with power, and they find themselves being transfigured into the same image from one degree of glory to another. Such a result can never be attained by bustling activity and elaborate organization. Only an attitude, like the artist's, of patient waiting and expectant contemplation can provide the channel for the Spirit's activity, and can result in the revelation of the divine glory. Thus relationship, viewed from this angle, means patient dependence and willingness to receive, coupled with an earnest concentration upon, and an outgoing of, the whole personality towards the Other with whom the relationship is effected. Given such conditions, the activity of the Spirit is assured. Both the individual and the community will advance towards the goal of becoming conformed to the likeness of Him who is the image of the invisible God.

IV

As we draw our study to a close, we do well to remind ourselves that the receiving of the Spirit is no light and easy thing : it cannot be contemplated without deep seriousness and concern. Archbishop Temple has brought this forcibly to our attention in one of his devotional studies of St. John's Gospel. " How dread a Companion and Guide," he writes, " is this Comforter ! We are distressed about some special fault, and ask His aid to overcome it ; whereupon He tells us that our real trouble is our self-complacence and self-reliance, and if it is His help that we seek, He will rouse us from these. But we do not want that at all ! Indeed our chief reason for wanting to overcome that special fault was that it disturbed our self-complacence, which we hoped, after a little moral effort, to enjoy once more. Or we seek His aid in living according to our standard of righteousness and are told that this standard is hardly worth striving after ; only the total committal of ' ourselves, our souls and bodies, to be a reasonable, holy and lively sacrifice ', is real righteousness. Or we turn to Him to be our Paraclete, our advocate, in the judgment ; and He tells us that we are judged already by our steady preference of our way to God's.

When we pray ' Come, Holy Ghost, our souls inspire ', we had better know what we are about. He will not carry us to easy triumphs and gratifying successes; more probably He will set us to some task for God in the full intention that we shall fail, so that others, learning wisdom by our failure, may carry the good cause forward. He may take us through loneliness, desertion by friends, apparent desertion even by God; that was the way Christ went to the Father. He may drive us into the wilderness to be tempted of the devil. He may lead us from the Mount of Transfiguration (if He ever lets us climb it) to the hill that is called the Place of a Skull. For if we invoke Him, it must be to help us in doing God's will, not ours; we cannot call upon the

> Creator Spirit, by whose aid
> The world's foundations first were laid

in order to use omnipotence for the supply of our futile pleasures or the success of our futile plans. If we invoke Him, we must be ready for the glorious pain of being caught by His power out of our petty orbit into the eternal purposes of the Almighty, in whose onward sweep our lives are as a speck of dust. The soul that is filled with the Spirit must have become purged of all pride or love of ease, all self-complacence and self-reliance; but that soul has found the only real dignity, the only lasting joy. Come then, Great Spirit, come. Convict the world; and convict my timid soul."

At the same time, as has been recognized throughout Christian history, the coming of the Comforter also means healing and joy and love. In St. Paul's great prayer of *Ephesians* 3, this fact is expressed in lyrical terms. He prays that the Ephesian Christians may so be strengthened with might by God's Spirit that they, being rooted and grounded in love, may comprehend with all saints what is the length and breadth and depth and height, and may know the love of Christ which passeth knowledge and be filled with all the fullness of God. The ancient hymn used in the Service for the Ordination of Priests also dwells upon the joys and blessings which the coming of the Spirit may mean to faithful souls.

Thou art the very Comforter
   In grief and all distress ;
The heav'nly gift of God most high,
   No tongue can it express ;
The fountain and the living spring
   Of joy celestial ;
The fire so bright, the love so sweet,
   The Unction spiritual.

Thou in Thy gifts art manifold,
   By them Christ's Church doth stand :
In faithful hearts thou writ'st thy law,
   The finger of God's hand.
O Holy Ghost, into our minds
   Send down thy heav'nly light
Kindle our hearts with fervent zeal,
   To serve God day and night.

Grant us the grace that we may know
   The Father of all might,
That we of his beloved Son
   May gain the blissful sight ;
And that we may with perfect faith
   Ever acknowledge thee,
The Spirit of Father, and of Son,
   One God in Persons Three.

Convicter and Comforter, Destroyer and Upbuilder, Purifier and Sanctifier, Ruler and Lover—such is the Holy Spirit. Yet, in the last resort, His aim is ever to glorify Christ in us and to lift us into the full enjoyment of our fellowship in the love of God.

Let us conclude with some words of St. Augustine, remembering that it is of the gift of the Spirit that he writes :

" In Thy gift we rest; there we enjoy Thee.

Our rest is our place. Love lifts us up thither,

And Thy good Spirit lifteth our lowliness from the gates of death.

" We are inflamed by Thy gift and we are borne aloft. We glow as we go. We mount up along the ascents of the heart and we sing the Song of the Ascents. By Thy fire, Thy good fire, we are enkindled and we proceed since we go up to the peace of Jerusalem.

For I was glad when they said unto me ' Let us go unto the house of the Lord '. There hath Thy good pleasure placed us, that we may desire no other thing than to dwell there for ever."[1]

[1] *Confessions*, XIII, 9 : 10.

INDEX

H

Habūrāh, Koinonia, in the New Testament, 74
Haggai, Book of, 99
Harrison, J. E.: *Ancient Art and Ritual*, 98
Headingley Lectures, 56
Hebrews, Epistle to, 31, 89, 116
Hinduism, *Rita* in, 70-1
' Holy ', meaning of, 19
Horton, W. M.: *Our Eternal Contemporary*, 22
Hoskyns, Edwyn, Sir: *Cambridge Sermons*, 11, 20
Howard, W. F.: *Christianity According to St. John*, 92, 94
Hoyle, Birch, Holy Spirit in St. Paul, 13
Hunter, A. M.: *Paul and his Predecessors*, 32-3

I

Individual, the, disappearance of in modern society, 67
Inspiration, as work of the Spirit, 96-7
Iran, *Asha* in, 71
Iroquois Indians, 54
Isaiah, Book of, 27-8, 29, 40, 73

J

Jephthah, 56
Jeremiah, Book of, 73
Joel, 33
John, St., Gospel according to, 30, 33, 45, 75, 91-3, 99, 110
Joseph, son of Jacob, 87
Joshua, 73
Judaism, apocalyptic movement in, 27
Judges, Book of, 56, 73

K

Koinonia, meaning of, 74-8, 81, 114

L

Lamont, Daniel: *Christ and the World of Thought*, 101
Law, the, importance of in Old Testament religion, 25-6, 103
— in the life of Saul of Tarsus, 42-3
Lewis, C. S.: *The Abolition of Man*, 71

Life, meaning of, 36-8
—, primitive ideas of, 39-40
—, Old Testament view of, 40-1
—, New Testament view of, 42-6
—, dependence of upon relation, 46-9, 106-8, 116-7
— regarded as a unity, 46, 49-50
Love, the Spirit manifested as, 50
Luke, St., Gospel according to, 57, 59, 75, 102

M

Ma'at, 71
Macdonald, A. J.: *The Interpreter Spirit and Human Life*, 90
MacMurray, John, Professor: *This Changing World*, 68-9, 83
Mana, meaning of, 54, 55
Manitu, meaning of, 54
Mannheim, Karl, Professor: *Diagnosis of our Time*, 67
Mark, St., Gospel according to, 57, 111
Matter, as opposed to Spirit, 11-13
Matthew, St., Gospel according to, 57
Messiah, the, coming of, 27-9
—, link of Messianic community with, 31-2
— in the writings of St. Paul, 32-4
—, resurrection of, 59
—, victory of over evil, 61-2
Micah, Book of, 56
Mishpat, 71, 72
Moffatt, Dr.: *Commentary on Epistles to the Corinthians*, 77-8, 94-5
Moses, 73, 92, 95
Murry, Middleton: *Heaven and Earth*, 78

N

Needham, Joseph, Dr.: *This Changing World*, 37-8
—, *Time: The Refreshing River*, 38-9
Nephesh, meaning of, 24
New Testament, references to the Spirit in, 27-34
Nicodemus, 104
Numbers, Book of, 72

O

Oldham, Dr.: *Christian News-Letter*, 52-3
Old Testament, references to the Spirit in, 25-7

124